Santa Claus

We are all afraid to talk about that dreaded subject … death, especially if you add the unthinkable … the death of a child. Why does our society fear death? Is our physical world and spiritual world divided into two parts, "black" and "white"? Why are we supposed to move on with our lives after a death? We are told that love is a form of energy, and energy never dies, it just exists in a different form after death.

I remember one Christmas Eve the anger in my mother's voice when I announced that I had just changed my "Santa List" and wanted different toys. My mother led me down the hallway into her bedroom, closed the door behind her and said, "There is no Santa Claus. I'm Santa and you cannot change your list!" From that time on I have always been a little leery about opening myself up to the unknown. I wanted to believe that there is a better life after our physical life; but it was not until my daughter, Cathy's death, that made me a believer in the everlasting life.

Hopefully, this book will make you a believer too, because it is not just my daughter's communications but a group of spirits that call themselves, "The Big Circle" which has merged together in joining spiritual and the physical worlds into a group called, "The Recording Circle – Bridge to the Afterlife. We, in the physical world have formed an international recording group out of love and we work to continue helping our loved ones grow in their new world.

God has given us hope and a new pathway for healing grief. This book will push every emotional button you have you will laugh, you will cry, but most of all, you will grow from this experience into a better person.

I'm Still Here

By
Martha Copeland

AA-EVP Publishing

PO Box 13111, Reno, Nevada 89507

www.aaevp.com

USA

First Edition

First Printing, 2005

This book is available from Internet book sellers and by order from local book stores. Signed copies are available from the author at www.evpcommunications.com and www.bigcircle.aaevp.com and by writing:

Martha Copeland
#191
6555 Sugarloaf Parkway, Suite 307
Duluth, GA 30097

catsstillhere@yahoo.com

[Please see order form at back of book]

ISBN 0-9727493-1-4

Cover design by Jody Rosen. Cover layout by Don Copeland

Printed in the United States on acid-free paper by Lightning Source, LaVergne, Tennessee, USA, www.lightningsource.com

Table of Contents

Part 1
Remembering Cathy ~ In This Life and Beyond

Part 2
The Big Circle Evolves

Part 3
Trying EVP for Yourself

Dedication

This book is dedicated in loving memory to my daughter Catherine Donna Amiss, my favorite "Cat." Thank you, Cathy, for all you've shown me, for continually taking me beyond the edges of my perception.

"From today's perspective, we can laugh at the ignorance of those poor souls whose lives were limited to sailing near the shore. We know now that the edge beyond which they feared to sail existed only in their beliefs; we can sail beyond the horizon without fear of what lies beyond. Knowledge of Earth's true nature gave us that freedom."

~ Bruce Moen

Foreword

Death is often spoken of as an abyss, a fearful void awaiting us after our last breath. In our culture, death is believed an ending beyond which no one is ever heard of again. Yet, you will see in Martha's story that just about everything you have been told about death is false. Death is, indeed, the end of a physical lifetime, but it is just a transition to another lifetime in a different aspect of the greater reality.

Martha's daughter, Cathy, has shown herself to be a wayshower, and just as Martha has become an inspiration here in the physical, Cathy has become an inspiration in her etheric world for all who have come to know her. We feel that Martha and Cathy's story, which is also the story of many others who are participating in this grand experience, is an illustration of the truth about "death" which we all must learn. We will survive the end of our physical body and continue to live in a different aspect of reality. And, if we try, we will be able to tell about it to those who remain in the physical.

There is abundant precedence for the communication described by Martha in *I'm Still Here*. People around the world have been using Electronic Voice Phenomena, or EVP, since the advent of electronic communication and recording devices to communicate with people on the "Other Side." Martha describes "The Big Circle" as a group of people in the etheric who are cooperating with one another to communicate with loved ones still in the physical. Other researchers have also reported such cooperation of a group of people in the etheric, making it clear that there is as much desire to communicate with loved ones across the veil expressed on the Other Side as is expressed here.

Other than helping to alleviate grief, communication across the veil may be intended to be a demonstration that we survive physical death. If so, the communication described in *I'm Still Here,* is probably the most important demonstration we are aware of employing EVP. You will see that Cathy is very prolific in her communication with Martha. You will also see that The Big Circle involves many loved ones on both sides of the veil, with numerous messages that provide both evidence and comfort.

As you read this book, take time to think of personal experiences that might have been intended as communication. Perhaps a strange phone call or something moved that once belonged to a loved one now "dead." Allow yourself to think that a loved one may be trying to communicate with you. See in this book that the members of The Big Circle are normal people and that there is no reason why you cannot experience similar communication. Allow yourself to at least tentatively accept the possibility that your loved ones who have "died" are still alive and interested in answering your call to communicate.

There are no guarantees that you will make contact with a particular person on the Other Side. There are so many reasons why you might not. But, as you will see in Martha and Cathy's story, it is possible and reasonable for you to try.

As a final note, and before we step aside so that you may learn about The Big Circle, we wish to thank Cathy and the others in the etheric for their patience with us on "this side," and for being way-showers. We also want to thank the members of the Recording Circle—Bridge to the Afterlife on this side for being so open to sharing their experiences with the world. To all of you, these are exciting times and your work will have profound meaning for all who are willing to see.

Tom and Lisa Butler
AA-EVP Directors

Introduction

As I was struggling to write this introduction, an email arrived in my inbox containing one of those stories that get passed on despite its unknown origin. Although written anonymously, it was ideally meant for me:

> Being a veterinarian, I had been called to examine a ten-year-old blue heeler named Belker. The dog's family—husband Ron, wife Lisa, and little boy Shane—were all very attached to Belker, and they were hoping for a miracle. I examined Belker and found he was dying of cancer. I told the family there were no miracles left for Belker and offered to perform the euthanasia procedure for the old dog in their home.
>
> As we made arrangements, Ron and Lisa told me they thought it would be good for the four-year-old Shane to observe the procedure. They felt Shane could learn something from the experience. The next day I felt the familiar catch in my throat as Belker's family surrounded him. Petting the old dog for the last time, Shane seemed so calm that I wondered if he understood what was going on. Within a few minutes, Belker slipped peacefully away. The little boy seemed to accept Belker's transition without any difficulty or confusion.
>
> We sat together for a while after Belker's death wondering aloud about the sad fact that animal lives are usually shorter than human lives. Shane, who had been listening quietly, piped up. "I know why," he said. Startled, we all turned to him. What came out of his mouth next stunned me. I'd never heard a more comforting explanation.
>
> He said, "Everybody is born so that they can learn how to live a good life, like loving everybody and being nice, right? Well," he continued, "animals already know how to do that, so they don't have to stay as long."
>
> Unknown Author

I smiled and paused as I read this, feeling tears well up in my eyes. I could relate to this story in so many ways. My daughter, Cathy, had passed in a car accident nearly three years earlier, at age twenty. Perhaps she had already learned how to live a good life. The little boy in the story showed a deep acceptance. I, too, have learned to be accepting of the staggering grief that comes with losing someone close. In fact, as a result of my experiences since Cathy's death, I have learned that there is a Divine Wisdom behind it all. My grief has caused me to grow spiritually, to feel compassion deeply, to understand life broadly. New and wonderful friendships have been forged, because this tragedy opened doors that would never before have existed. I have found comfort in knowing that Cathy is still present in my life; she just exists in a different form.

After Cathy's death, my husband and I went to see a presentation by the famous medium, George Anderson, and to get a private reading from him. In the midst of that reading, he said, "Your daughter is telling me that if she were to go to Mongolia, she would find her way back." Cathy has done just that: She has found her way back to us.

This book was created to tell the story of Cathy's continual presence in my life, both before and since her death. It tells how she has introduced me to many other grieving parents longing to connect with their children as I had connected with Cathy. It tells the story of The Big Circle of Life which extends far beyond our sensory perceptions to something indeed extrasensory.

Simply stated, our loved ones have been communicating to us from the Other Side. By using Electronic Voice Phenomena (EVP), we can talk to them and hear from them, sometimes often. Engaging in this activity led to the formation of our powerful support group, Recording Circle—Bridge to the Afterlife. This group is another example of the good which has come from my loss. It is full of brave and open-minded people with one common goal: to continue communications with loved ones now in Spirit. We do this out of love and a desire to perpetuate the spiritual growth in which we all are immersed. Those who participate in Recording Circle—Bridge to the Afterlife are truly spiritual pioneers of our time.

By sharing these stories of our journeys, I hope to give you, the reader, a meaningful experience. I've also included resources and considerable how-to information in case you'd like to try this type of communication yourself. Here's hoping that this book somehow manages to deliver ways to access the message your loved ones in Spirit may long to send: *"I'm still here."*

About the Author

Martha P. Copeland was born in Columbia, South Carolina, and reared in both Hampton and Newport News, Virginia. She now resides in Lawrenceville, Georgia.

When Martha was six years old, complete deafness in her left ear was discovered, and she had very little hearing in her right ear. This disability may be one reason Martha learned to rely on the *inner voice* inside her head. This defect was corrected with surgery, and she now regards that early disability as a special gift. Furthermore, she attributes this as the major factor in her spirituality.

Cathy's death has shaped her life around a passionate purpose: a devotion to finding a doorway to the Other Side and helping others through their grief with lessons from spirit.

Acknowledgements

I would like to give special thanks to my loving, supportive family and friends. The labor of love is a powerful healing tool.

Especially:

- ♥ My husband, Don Copeland, for his labor of love in sustaining my spirit, building the meditation room, and formatting the book cover.

- ♥ My sisters, Donna Sloan and Ginny Sawyer, for their ideas, helpful opinions, and stories for my book.

- ♥ My niece, Rachel Sawyer, Cathy's cousin and best friend, without whose determination and persistence this book would not have been possible.

- ♥ My nephew, Todd Sloan, who designed the website for Cathy's book and who (according to Cathy) understood her better then anyone else.

- ♥ My parents, Don and Sallie Pierce.

- ♥ My son, Robert Marek Amiss.

- ♥ My nephews, Brad Sloan and Jamie Sawyer, for their stories.

- ♥ Sarah Estep, the true founder and pioneer of EVP and the AA-EVP.

- ♥ Lisa and Tom Butler, Directors of the AA-EVP, whose encouragement and support inspired me every step of the way.

- ♥ Jillene Moore, who organized and structured all the many stories so my story could be told.

- ♥ Jody Rosen, who created a masterpiece for the book cover, her husband Jim and their son Justin for making my dream of having Cathy's photo on the book cover complete.

♥ Lisa Yesse, with the assistance of Cheryl Bain, in designing and creating the "Big Circle" Website for our group.

♥ Martha Knolling, my editor, who lived with the manuscript during Thanksgiving and the Christmas season and considered it a privilege to be part of the project.

♥ Irene and Mike Matzgannis, my dearest friends.

♥ George Wynne, my dear supportive friend for his wise advice.

♥ **All those who participate in the Recording Circle—Bridge to the Afterlife ...** specially, Karen Mossey, my good friend and co-pilot, Judy Quillen, Kathy Malone, and Jo Anne Winsor.

♥ **The Big Circle** including Cathy and her friends on the Other Side, who played a huge role in gathering the resources for this book, without whom I could not have told their story.

The Book Cover
By Jody Rosen

Martha and Jody Rosen in St. Maarten

Jody Sweet Rosen was born outside of San Francisco, spending the summers in Carmel. She lived in Carmel and the Big Sur Mountains during her early twenties, where she met her husband, Jim. They purchased land in Northern California where their son, Justin, was born. In 1985, after ten years, they moved to the Caribbean Island of St. Maarten.

Jody was drawn to the arts early on. She started sewing, playing the flute and piano at the age of nine. She trained with a chef in Carmel and worked in some of the finest restaurants in her late teens. She began china painting and belly dancing in California while working at the Community School. When she moved to the Caribbean she built a small café and successfully ran it for six years. Jody began painting with oils in 1991. Her love for the expression in painting expanded to pastels, watercolors and acrylics. She enjoys doing pottery by hand as well as painting and glazing ceramics. For the last few years, she has been painting on small canvases, and been incorporating her painting with sewing, doing hand painted pockets for tote bags. Jody recently started doing some larger pieces on stretched canvas.

The turquoise waters and tropical vegetation of her island inspire her. She lives perched above the sea with an expansive view of neighboring islands. She currently owns a small convenience store and does the time-share sales at the Belair Beach Hotel. She enjoys swimming, running and dance. Her loves in life are her husband, son, her three dogs and one cat, the freedom of painting, sewing, making pottery and gardening.

Did The Big Circle Pick Jody?

While vacationing in St. Maarten, we attended the orientation provided by the hotel for newly arrived guests. It offered information on the island as well as opportunities to sign up for excursions. The orientation was presented by several people, each explaining what their function was to make our stay comfortable and fun. One attractive lady, Jody Rosen, was a local artist and has a small gift shop at the hotel. As soon as Jody started speaking, I heard a voice inside my head saying, "She's the one!" I whispered to my sister, Donna, "Hey I wonder if she would do the book cover?" Donna glanced back at me with a look saying, "Yeah, dream on!" After the orientation was over, I approached Jody and told her about the book and what the contents were. Jody expressed to me that she had an interest in the paranormal and suffered a tragic loss in her family as well. Jody's ten-year-old niece was killed by an automobile while riding her bicycle. My connection to Jody, and why I felt that she was the one to create the book cover, did not fully occur to me until she asked me to contact her at the room number 222. I knew then that my meeting Jody was not by mere "chance," and had been made first on a spiritual level. The significance of the number 222 relates to Judy Quillen, one of the mothers in our Recording Circle – Bridge to the Afterlife. Judy's daughter, Jamie's favorite number was 222 and this is one of her spiritual signs to her mother.

Donna and I thought Jody was very gifted and talented with a wonderful warm personality. We had hoped she would agree and also that her price would be affordable for my budget. Jody called me on the next to last day of my stay and we discussed the details of her working on the book cover and what her fee would be for her service. Jody told me she would do it for free and I just could not believe it! The day we were checking out of the hotel I met with Jody again and she showed me this amazing drawing she was already working on for the book. The drawing reflected perfectly what I had envisioned it should look like.

I asked Jody if I could include her web address on the web site for the book, *"I'm Still Here."* Due to her unique talent, other people may be interested in her work. Jody seems to posses a natural intuition allowing her to create pictures that capture the essence of our loved one's personality just through her artwork.

Jody mentioned to me as we were leaving for the airport, "Don't you think it is strange that you have rented the identical vehicle that I own?

Jody loves animals and the ocean just as Cathy did.

This is Jody's first book cover and my first book. I think The Big Circle had a hand in making this all come together.

Part 1

Remembering Cathy ~
In This Life and Beyond

The Workshop

I'm not sure how I got here in front of this room full of people in a hotel in Reno, Nevada. Lisa Butler, co-director of the American Association of Electronic Voice Phenomena (AA-EVP), asked me if I would teach a class about grieving parents who have used EVP to contact their deceased children, and somehow I agreed.

I am one of those parents, and I told myself I needed to just make it through this gig without crying. I've never done anything like this, and it doesn't help my nervousness to have a film crew from Universal Studios in the back of the room with their cameras pointed at me. My sister, Ginny, and my friend, Karen Mossey, are here in the room, too, lending their support. And how we all got here is the story I'm about to tell.

Every face in the room is focused on me, and all seem to be interested in what I have to say. This is stunning! I'm wearing a T-shirt which one of my grieving mother's friends gave to me. It has on it the picture of my daughter Cathy, who died at age twenty, December 23, 2001—two days before Christmas.

I hear myself telling the audience that, after Cathy's death, I tried everything I could think of, such as grief therapy and anti-depressants, to get through the darkness. "But the first time I heard Cathy's voice after her death, saying these words, *'I'm still here,'*" I told them, "I felt hope. The path to my recovery opened up." I told the group that it is my hope they will find in this workshop a tool to help themselves, or someone they know, in the grief recovery process.

After my introduction, Karen got up to tell the story of how we met. Once I began to pick up Cathy's voice, I went to the Internet to find other parents who might be hearing from their children on electronic devices. I found the AA-EVP, and Karen was a member. When I contacted her, she offered to call and talk to me. She had lost her son, Rob, to a brain seizure. We found so many similarities between our respective children. Karen still relates that she felt a "driving force" to know more about Cathy.

Karen came to my home in Atlanta from her home in New Hampshire to get to know more about our story. You'll read in future chapters about many dreams, synchronicities and messages that we have shared involving Rob or Cathy or both. Since these early days, and because of some amazing events, we've become close friends.

I have planned this whole ninety-minute workshop carefully, since Karen has told me she didn't really want to be an integral part of the workshop planning and delivery. I'm a little shaky about how things might go, but something in my heart spurs me on.

I've already talked about the stories of how I first began communicating with Cathy, and how I joined with others and formed our Recording Circle—Bridge to the Afterlife group. I've told the crowd that no special equipment is needed for a loved one to contact you. For us, Cathy's voice came the first time through Windows Media Player on my niece, Rachel's, computer. I've told them that when Cathy visits me in dreams, I know when it's a 'visitation' dream because she is aglow. I've talked about the importance of relaxation when one records EVP, and now I'm about to launch into exercises and techniques one can use to begin to do EVP recording. I hope you'll join us on this journey!

The Miracle of Marek

Riding in my sister's car and listening to the swish of the windshield wipers, I started thinking back. It's another time, much like this....

I am sitting in the hospital trauma room, surrounded by the trauma team with a parade of doctors popping in and out. I keep repeating the mantra, "I believe in miracles, I believe in miracles, I believe in miracles...."

Within this reverie, I reflect on several earlier miracles, perhaps the truest miracle of all being the day Cathy was born. I remember my doctor dancing around the delivery room, saying, "Our miracle baby has arrived!" Cathy had beaten the odds predicted by many specialists. (Some of these odds I have kept hidden from the doctors even today.)

After seven years of marriage, I discussed my desire to have a baby with my husband Robert. We had purchased our second home and it was large enough and located in a nice neighborhood. Robert was doing well in his job, making it possible for me to stay home with the baby. Robert was not keen on the idea of having children, because he felt it would interfere with our free lifestyle (getting away on weekends and skiing trips in the winter). We had dated five years before getting married, yet somehow had failed to discuss how we felt about having children. I had just assumed this was a natural progression of the marriage experience.

I came from a family of four children (two sisters and a brother) so I could not imagine not having children of my own. Even as a young child, I loved baby dolls and treated them like they were real (even washing their hair until it was matted and sticking straight up on their heads). Interestingly, my sisters, Ginny and Donna, never cared for baby dolls. For me, however, the maternal instinct was always strong.

After much discussion, I was finally able to convince Robert to let me have a baby.

Never in my wildest dreams could I imagine having any difficulty in conceiving a baby. The thought of such a possibility never once entered my mind. After all, everything else in my life was going according to plan. I had married my high school sweetheart. We both had good jobs, and we had purchased a large house. Of course, the next phase of our marriage would be a baby, which should just simply happen. My mother, my sister, Donna, and many of my friends had given birth to babies without any complications. Certainly, it would only be a matter of time before that baby stork would be visiting me. During this time, I enjoyed browsing through the baby departments of major stores and looking at all the darling little outfits and imagining how my baby would look in them. Each passing month I prayed and waited; each passing month brought disappointment.

Finally, my gynecologist referred us to the Medical College of Virginia. He believed that the staff there offered the most advanced technology for couples having fertility problems. In the early exploration of treatment for fertility, medical facilities were not sensitive to the needs of the man. Robert was instructed to pick up a container in a waiting room full of women, then retreat to the closest men's restroom and produce sperm. For him, this task was very humiliating and causing additional frustration in our marriage, which in turn, Robert would take out on me. We both began to feel more like guinea pigs and dreaded our upcoming doctor visits. After a two year period, the specialists at the Medical College of Virginia told us that it would be a miracle if we could ever have a baby of our own. Their suggestion was to contact an adoption agency. Robert was totally against the idea of adoption and felt that if it were "God's will," we would have a child of our own.

My mother told me about elderly Dr. Mitchell, still practicing medicine with a reputation for helping women with my problem. My mother had great faith in his abilities and from his record of success, she felt absolutely certain that he could help me. Dr. Mitchell had the reputation of performing miracles, which led my Aunt Frances to him. She was having problems conceiving a baby, but after seeking Dr. Mitchell's help, she eventually gave birth to four healthy boys. Once again, I had great hope for being able to have a baby and I found myself on "cloud nine" as my mother accompanied me to my appointment with Dr. Mitchell. En route I imagined Dr. Mitchell telling me, "Of course, you can have a baby. I see nothing wrong with you."

After completing my examination, Dr. Mitchell asked me to get dressed and join him in his office. Excited, I practically jumped back into my clothes, excited to hear his encouraging words. Entering his office, I noticed that my mother was already seated as Dr. Mitchell, with his head bent, examined my file. Removing his glasses, he rubbed his tired old eyes and looked up at my anxious face. In a shaky voice he told me what I did not want to hear: There were too many problems and I could never produce a baby of my own. Dr. Mitchell recommended adoption, but I knew that this was not an option for me.

Leaving Dr. Mitchell's office, my mother and I had to cross a busy highway and I remember my mother taking my hand as tears flowed down my face. Why couldn't an approaching car just hit me and set me free from this awful pain in my heart? At twenty- six, my life was over. My dreams of a family of my own would never happen. Life was not fair. My longing for a child consumed my every thought to the extent that I could even imagine that, while in a grocery store, taking a baby nestled in a carrier inside a shopping cart and running away with it. These women could have other babies; I could never have a child. I was a complete failure and my heart was broken. Often sitting in our upstairs bathroom and looking out the window overlooking our wooded backyard, I would cry in private.

One of these times I recall a beautiful warm light filling the bathroom, surrounding me. It felt as if some unseen force was hugging me. No words were spoken, but I *knew* everything would be all right, and the most calming sense of peace came over me. I would always be an aunt to Donna's son, Bradley, and my sister, Ginny, had just learned that she was expecting her first child. In fact, Donna lived down the street from me and I could frequently see Bradley, spoiling him and babysitting as often as possible. However, Vaughn, Donna's husband, was promoted in his job, which meant they would likely move out of the state. This was bittersweet news for me. On one hand, I was happy this would allow Donna to quit her job and stay home with Brad. On the other hand, I was deeply saddened knowing that I would no longer have my sister and adored nephew nearby.

My marriage to Robert had become one of convenience, yet we had been together since I was sixteen years old and he, twenty. We shared a history together, despite the difficulties in our marriage. I knew this change in our family dynamic would intensify the disappointment I already felt toward my marriage.

After Donna and her family moved, I missed seeing Brad and my yearning for a child consumed me. Sensing my despair, my mother offered to share the expense of the adoption. Although financial reasons were not preventing us from adopting a baby, her offer still gave me the courage to broach the subject with Robert again.

Ultimately, Robert and I reached an agreement that once the adoption was finalized and if he still had doubts, we would part. He would be free from any obligations to the child. After establishing this understanding with him, I then contacted the Catholic Home in Hampton, Virginia, to start the adoption process.

We were assigned a caseworker by the name of Sally, which just

Sally with baby Marek on her lap

happens to be my mother's name (except she spells her name "Sallie"). Sally phoned us to set up an appointment to meet us and inspect our home. I cleaned every inch, crack and corner of my house, including all of the closets and drawers. Even my little miniature long-haired dachshund, Gretel, was spotless. No little spider web would prevent us from qualifying for adoption. Sally arrived and walked briefly through our house, not once opening a closet or a drawer. Sitting at our kitchen table, Sally explained the adoption process as we completed the required paperwork. My heart sank when Sally mentioned that the waiting time for a healthy baby could take three to five years.

Six months after our first interview, Sally called us with the news that our waiting time would be much less than expected. This happy development inspired us to get the nursery all ready. My sister Ginny's husband, Steve, offered to paint a large cartoon character of a lion on one of the nursery walls, adding the finishing touch to the room. Later, when my baby was with us, I loved coming home from work and rocking in the chair my mother had given me. I would play the little musical toy mobile that hung over the crib while rearranging the items on the changing table. Sometimes I felt that the cartoon lion on the wall would wink at me in a reassuring way, letting know me that he would watch over and protect my baby.

While going through the adoption process I was reunited with a friend from high school named Lisa. She and her husband happened to be adopting a baby from the same agency. This was exciting because now I had someone who could share my experiences with this ordeal.

Sally contacted me to inform us that we were the proud parents of a baby girl and could pick her up in one week. Excitedly, I begged her to describe our baby and give me all the details. What does she look like? Does she smile often? How much does she weigh? What foods does she eat? Sally told me she had black hair and huge blue eyes with a tiny mole on the right corner of her mouth. I immediately called Lisa expecting her to share in my excitement. Her reaction was a far cry from what I expected. Lisa was furious, reminding me that she had applied to adopt before we had.

The next day I received a call from Sally offering her apology. Regrettably, the birth mother had decided to keep her baby. Sally then requested that I not share information with other couples working through the agency.

One week later, Lisa telephoned me inviting me over to see her baby girl. Arriving at Lisa's with stuffed animals and a little pink dress, I noticed that the baby's hair was black. She had huge blue eyes with a tiny mole on the right corner of her mouth. Holding the baby in my arms, I could not help feeling that this was the same baby Sally had first called me about.

Returning home, I entered the waiting nursery, touching every item, all in perfect order for my baby. Sitting in the rocking chair, longing to lull my baby girl to sleep, I could feel tears streaming down my cheeks. I sat there until the sunlight faded from the room. The cartoon lion on the wall seemed to be calling out to me, "Better luck next time, kiddo," and I watched him until he faded into the darkness of the night. Sadly, I had come to the conclusion that God did not want me to have children, and my beloved little dachshund, Gretel, would remain my only baby.

Nine months passed. As we were getting ready to attend Robert's Hampton High School reunion, the phone rang. It was Sally inviting me to pick up my baby boy on Monday. Given our previous disappointment, we became a bit apprehensive and grappled with mixed emotions. At the reunion many classmates brought their children with them and asked Robert if he had children. Proudly, he announced that we had a boy named Marek.

Marek and the Tiger

Very little information was made available to us about the baby. We did know his age (two months) and that his mother was stationed at Langley Air Force Base, Virginia, where she worked with computers. She liked to play the piano. Sally described her as a petite blonde with a little turned- up nose. Her father was a minister somewhere in the "Deep South," and she had kept the baby's birth a secret from her family and the natural father. While home on leave, she had conceived the baby with an old boyfriend who liked to work on cars. She did love him, but felt that they were both too young to marry, and she wanted her son to have a good home.

Marek's birthmother made the unselfish decision to give him up for adoption, and because of her decision, I am forever grateful to her. I later explained to Marek how much his birthmother loved him. I wanted Marek to appreciate her courage and compassion.

My philosophy on adoption is best expressed in this poem published in a "Dear Abby" newspaper column. I, of course, saved this for my miracle Marek.

Legacy of an Adopted Child

Once there were two women
  who never knew each other.
One you do not remember,
  the other you call mother.
Two different lives
  shaped to make yours one.
One became your guiding star,
  the other became your sun.
The first gave you life
  and the second taught you to live in it.
The first gave you a need for love,
  and the second was there to give it.
One gave you a nationality,
  the other gave you a name.
One gave you the seed of talent,
  the other gave you an aim.
One gave you emotions,
  the other calmed your fears.
One saw your first sweet smile,
  the other dried your tears.
One gave you up ...
  it was all she could do.
The other prayed for a child
  and God led her straight to you.
And now you ask me through your tears,
  the age-old question unanswered through the years ...
Heredity or environment ...
  which are you the product of?
Neither, my darling ... neither,
  just two different kinds of love.

Author Unknown

My sister Ginny gave me this darling little sailor suit (perfectly apt as he now serves in the Navy) to fit a three-month-old baby. I anticipated the outfit would be too large for him since he was only two months, but I would put it on him anyway to avoid hurting Ginny's feelings.

I envisioned my tiny Gerber baby and how adorable he would look in his sailor outfit. Sally told us we could pick up our baby at 4:00 P.M. on Monday at the Catholic Home Agency. Several times during the day I drove passed the agency like a stalker, hoping to catch a glimpse of Sally carrying my son into the building.

Marek and the Gretel

Robert came home at 3:00 P.M. and we headed to the Catholic Home with Gretel, the diaper bag, sailor outfit and toys in tow. I felt like I was floating and wanted to fly out of my body and zoom ahead of all the traffic. Every stoplight seemed like hours instead of minutes and our car seemed to attract every Sunday driver in front of it. Once we arrived at the agency, Sally greeted us at the door and led us into her small office. On the floor lying on a blanket was the biggest, ugliest baby I had ever seen. We looked down at this huge baby with bluish skin tone and a bright red strawberry between his eyes. His head had an odd shape and his body was big and flat with two long skinny legs hanging out of the diapers. My first impression was that he resembled the comedian, John Candy. Sally left us with the baby in private as she closed the door to her office. Speechless, Robert and I remained in our chairs staring down at our baby. Breaking the silence,

Robert asked me, "Hey, couldn't you tell them you would like to wait for the next one?" As he spoke, I happened to notice a small device, which resembled a tape recorder resting on the desk. I became concerned that our conversation was being taped and replied, "Oh, this is our boy!" I then tried to squeeze his bountiful body (the size of a six-month-old) into the sailor suit made for a three-month-old baby. What a challenge! The top was so tight that his arms could not rest beside his body, leaving his stomach exposed. The only way I could get the bottom of the outfit on him was to keep the snaps completely un-snapped. All the while, it occurred to me that the many baby clothes previously purchased would have to be exchanged.

As we left the agency with our baby, Sally stopped to introduce us to the director of the adoption agency. Walking down the stairs, all ninety pounds of my four foot, eleven inch frame tried desperately to hold on to this big baby without dropping him. Approaching our car, I could hear the director comment to Sally, "Boy, you really mis-matched them!"

Marek turned into a beautiful little boy and is now a handsome man. In fact, his appearance changed within weeks of coming home to us. His transformation reminds me of the story about the ugly duckling who turned into a beautiful swan. Robert and I loved Marek, and our love for him made us both want to work to improve our marriage.

My Grandfather Pierce lived in Smithfield, Virginia, and owned a lot of property surrounding a small lake. He offered each grandchild a piece of property on the lake to build a house and Robert wanted to take him up on his offer. I did not want to move because the property was very isolated and Marek would not have any friends nearby. However, when Ginny, her husband and their daughter Rachel (the same age as Marek) decided to build on the lake, Robert was able to talk me into it. I made him promise that in two years, if I was not happy, we would move back to the city. (In two years we did actually move back to the city when Cathy was only three weeks old.)

I took Rachel and Marek to pre-school everyday, because Ginny was expecting her second child and suffering from morning sickness. After school, I brought Rachel and Marek back to my house to play. In their conversations they addressed an invisible friend by the name of Tommy. I once asked the children who Tommy was and Rachel, turn-ing to me with a head full of curls in pigtails, smiled and said, "His name is Tommy and he used to live here a long time ago." Ginny also noticed the kids often talking to Tommy, but we felt he was an imaginary friend.

Many strange occurrences took place while living on the lake, and I was not alone in this observation. Ginny and my cousin Diane Hayes, who had also built on the lake, seemed to share these strange observations. For example, I would put down my hairbrush and turn briefly, only to notice that it was gone, but while searching for it, would find it in the exact spot again. Even when my grandmother was alive, she complain about similar strange happenings, but we were dismissive and blamed it on her age.

Once, after returning from dropping the kids off at pre-school, I decided to wash some clothes. My washer and dryer were located in our basement and I carried the load of clothes downstairs. In the kitchen, I had a small radio playing and decided to turn it off while I practiced my yoga and meditation. Going to the basement to put the clothes into the dryer I could hear music playing from the radio. I unplugged the radio thinking something might be wrong with it and went about my household duties. The buzzer from the dryer informed me that the clothes were ready and I went to retrieve them before they

Marek with Rachel and
Martha's Father, Donald

wrinkled. While folding the clothes in the basement, I could hear music playing again, but this time it was louder. I was alone in the house with the exception of my two dogs, one cat and my bird, Crackers.

Even today, I cannot find a logical explanation as to how the radio could turn on by itself or how it got plugged back into the socket.

My grandfather's property had a lot of history and perhaps this could explain some of the questions surrounding these strange occurrences. During the Revolutionary War and the Civil War, the soldiers camped around that lake. Cornwallis, the British military leader who commanded forces during the American Revolutionary War, had slept in an old house located near the lake and our property. Remains of an old house still stood on the property and this is where the children said Tommy had once lived. Ginny recalls once catching a glimpse of a small, red-haired boy wearing old dungarees, entering Rachel's bedroom. She peeked inside the bedroom, only to find Rachel alone and asleep in her bed. Ginny later mentioned the boy to Rachel and she replied, "It's only Tommy coming to visit me."

There were several instances when Rachel informed us that our mother was on her way to visit. My mother had not called and this was the pre-cell phone era, so we were unable to contact her. When my mother's car appeared in our lane, I turned to Rachel and ask, "How did you know this?" She gave me a frustrated look and replied, "Tommy told me." I often wonder if Tommy was the start of our "Big Circle." Perhaps he knew Cathy before we did.

My Miracle Baby

Martha six months pregnant with Cathy

Living in Smithfield was one of those strange periods of my life and it was unfortunately not good for our marriage, which was becoming increasingly unbearable. Robert had started staying in the city until late leaving me alone with Marek. In truth, we had a platonic relationship for several years, and there were other factors that led to a very stressful life together.

Eventually, we decided that it might be better for Marek if we ended our marriage. Then I had a strange dream exactly three weeks after John Lennon was murdered. I dreamt that John Lennon told me I was going to have a baby. This was really strange because George Harrison had always been my favorite Beatle. The dream startled me. When I awoke, I felt as if a large ball of light were glowing inside me and spreading around me like a bubble. I found myself floating down

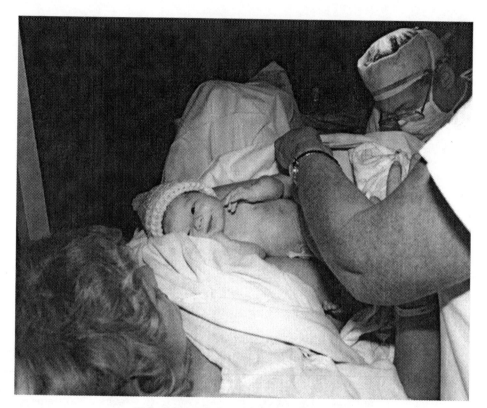

"My miracle baby arrives with a smile"

the hallway in our small den. I woke Robert and told him about it and
that is when our "Miracle Baby" began her journey to us.

Later, I thought of the whole dream as simply that—a dream.
Shortly afterwards, my sister, Ginny, told me that she had a dream that
I would have a girl. This is when we still resided as neighbors on the
property given to us by our grandfather. A narrow gravel lane ran in
front of our houses, and it is here that Ginny had seen the little blonde
girl in her dream. Ginny felt that they had been old friends in a previous time. The little girl walked up to her with a big grin on her face
and told her that she was coming back and I would be her mother. In
the dream both Ginny and the little girl were so excited about the
prospect.

About this time I started experiencing horrible nausea and vomit-
ing, morning sickness. However, I was sure it was some horrible dis-

ease, maybe even cancer. Apparently Ginny knew better. She showed up at my house one morning with one of those home pregnancy tests. I tested positive.

I visited my doctor for confirmation. A few days later his nurse called me and informed me that the test also showed positive. When I entered the office for my first follow-up appointment, my doctor and his staff cheered happily. Clapping their hands together, they sang, "This is going to be our miracle baby!"

Cathy's birth was easy. I visited the doctor on Friday, and on Monday I was scheduled to undergo a Caesarean section. Due to the baby's size, I was told that natural childbirth was impossibility for me so I prepared myself for the Caesarean. Saturday morning I went into labor and arrived at the hospital with my contractions only minutes apart. There wasn't enough time needed to perform a Caesarean. Cathy arrived just as I wished, by natural childbirth. She arrived with the most perfect timing—just before the cut-off that allowed me to receive my hospital dinner!

After Cathy's delivery, she was placed on my stomach. She looked up at me, her face beaming with a wide smile as she gazed into my face. My doctor continued to rejoice at the miracle of Cathy's birth, noting he had never before seen a baby smile like that just after being born. He told me, "It's as if she already knows you!" Luckily, this moment was captured by my husband's camera.

Had we known each other in a previous life? I remember once when Cathy was very young and holding onto her hand as we were walking. She looked up at me and grinned saying, "Mama, do you remember when I was the mama and you were my little girl?" Years later, she would often get frustrated with me not being able to operate our VCR and DVD players. Cathy would show me how to use these devices. However, I could never remember Cathy's instructions on operating this equipment. Cathy would take the controls away from me saying, "Sometimes I feel like the mother and you are my child!"

Now I am jerked away from that long ago moment, into another. I see two doctors approaching me in their green scrubs. They are telling me that it will be a miracle if Cathy survives. At six years old, a German shepherd mixed dog has attacked her. She was pretty much scalped with her head torn into chunks. I am informed that, in the event Cathy does make it, she may have brain damage. The dog had bitten through the skull into her brain.

It was just a couple of hours ago that I was driving Cathy and Marek to stay with their dad. Cathy was three and Marek was seven when Robert and I decided that it would be in their best interest if we divorced. Now, I am a single mother working in real estate and earning top sales status for my company. My broker has planned a dinner at the country club for the builders and their clients, and I am to present a speech. Cathy, now six, is crying in the car because she wants me to stay home and I am already stressed while trying to explain to her that this is a required part of my job. I stop in front of Robert's house and nearly push Cathy out the door toward her dad as she fights with me. Looking in my rear-view mirror, I see him holding her as she is still crying with her hand outstretched toward the direction of my moving car. Marek stands silently beside his dad and Cathy. He is such an easy child. I try to concentrate on my speech, but instead I find myself fighting back my tears.

Running late for the dinner, I pull into the parking lot and dash into the country club. A waiter stops me to ask if I am Martha Amiss and hands me a phone. Robert is on the line and tells me that he is at the hospital with Cathy and explains that the neighbor's dog has bitten her and wants me to meet him there. Traveling to the hospital I am thinking about a dog bite to the hand and perhaps a couple of stitches necessary. Entering the emergency entrance, I am greeted by three ladies with the trauma team who would like to talk to me before I see Cathy. Annoyed by their delaying me, I follow them to a small office. They tell me that Cathy's injuries are critical and want to prepare me for what I would see. Even with their warning I scream falling to my knees when I see Cathy. I remember turning to Robert and crying, "She'll never be normal again. How could this happen so soon after my just leaving?" Cathy is unconscious, unaware of what is taking place. My parents stop by briefly and not realizing the seriousness of her condition, leave to go on a cruise. I call Ginny and my sister Donna, now residing in Charleston, South Carolina, to inform them of the shattering news. Feeling alone and scared, I am suddenly overwhelmed with guilt as I remember Cathy's behavior in my car, the way she desperately wanted to stay with me. If only I had just stayed home with Cathy and Marek, everything would be all right. If only my regular babysitter had not been sick, the kids would both be safe and in their own beds. If only I had made an excuse to my broker, another agent could have delivered the speech. If only ….

Donna arrives the next day and her support is much needed. She has contacted my priest, Winn Lewis of Saint Mark's Episcopal Church, where I have attended since age twelve. A prayer chain for Cathy's recovery has started. During this time I just remain in a daze, going home only to shower and feed the animals. My house seems to overflow with family or friends waiting there for me, and I want them to go away. I do not have time for conversations and do not want to discuss Cathy's condition.

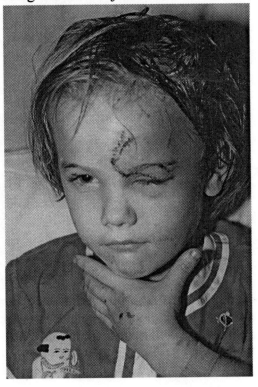

Standing in ICU watching Cathy's unconscious form, I wonder if she will ever come out of this coma. Nurses stop by and plead with me to go home and rest. My response is the same. "I believe in miracles and the healing power of a mother." A nurse hands me a cup of coffee and yet again, my shaky hand spills the coffee on Cathy. The nurse again runs to wipe

Cathy recovering from dog attack

off Cathy and again asks me to leave. Just as I pick up my purse to leave, I hear Cathy's squeaky little voice calling out to me, "Mama, I have to go use the potty." I look down and stare into the face of my miracle child. The cramped, curtained room is filled with doctors and nurses as word spreads throughout the hospital of this miracle. Cathy escapes this ordeal without much noticeable, permanent damage, either mental or physical.

My friend, Irene Matzgannis, comes to the hospital to help me pack Cathy's things and take her home. Her hospital room resembles a toy

Cathy and Marek

department filled with gifts from friends and people who have heard about her accident through the media. There is a small red wagon given to Cathy by the paramedics who rescued her after her accident. Irene and I make several trips carrying the gifts to my house to make room for Cathy in my car. On our last trip we put Cathy into the wagon surrounding her with the remaining stuffed animals. Cathy's head is still swollen, making her look like a surreal monster instead of my six-year-old daughter. Her scalp has been stapled together and her matted hair reminds me of some of my old baby dolls. As we pull the wagon down the hospital hallway, the nurses run to say goodbye to Cathy. She has become very popular during her stay. Heading toward the elevator, the wagon suddenly flips over and Cathy falls backwards, hitting her head on the floor. Nurses swarmed around her and one snaps at me, "What are you trying to do, kill her?" I am upset; they are upset. Irene's normally olive complexion turns several shades of red. Cathy is okay and just smiles, asks if I would rent her favorite videos,

Ole Yeller and *Rin Tin Tin*. Surprisingly enough, these movies are about large dogs. (Cathy never did develop a fear of dogs of any size and cried when she found out the dog that had bitten her had been put to sleep.)

Cathy with Irene at the falls

Several nurses assist us in helping Cathy into the back of my car. Irene tells me that she will follow me home in her car so she can help me situate Cathy and unload the rest of her things. Driving home a car careens into my lane, causing me to go up on the curb to avoid a collision. This sends all the stuffed toys airborne with several hitting me in the back of my head. The other car continues, not even stopping. Luckily, Cathy is safely strapped into the backseat and she laughs at all of this. Once home, we get Cathy settled into her bed and I pop in the videos for her to watch. Irene and I are still frazzled and she suggests having a glass of wine to calm our nerves. Looking in my refrigerator I'm not sure if I have any wine because it has been weeks since I've gone to a grocery store. In the very back I spot a bottle with just enough to fill two small wine glasses. Even though it is January, it is warm and we go outside on my patio as Irene makes a toast, "To no more bad luck." As we clink our wine glasses together, tiny cracks form in both glasses, spilling our wine onto the patio floor. No more bad luck? So ....

My flood of memories ceases. Now I am back in the present moment, riding with my sister, watching the rain drizzle down, stuck in Christmas traffic. My cell phone rings again. It is the hospital again, asking me to get there as quickly as possible. They inform me to notify family members to meet me at the hospital. Looking out the window, I think about Cathy's nickname, Cat, and wonder to myself, "Has my Cat run out of lives?"

Donna is rambling on about how she hopes Cathy won't have to be in a large cast for Christmas. If that's the case, she says, I could just let her stay downstairs. My husband, Don, would have to carry Cathy upstairs for me to bathe her. I look at the SUV ahead as it stops at the light with a Christmas tree strapped to the top and reply, "No, Cathy's dead."

I can still see those two doctors dressed in green scrubs telling me how hard they had worked to save her, how terribly sorry they were for me.

Just Before the End

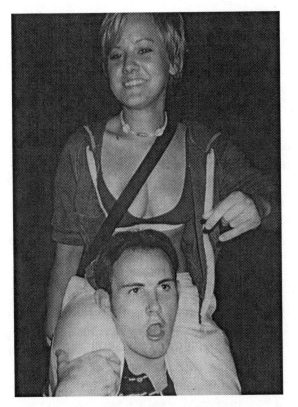

Cathy with friend, Matt, in 2000

In mid-November 2001, Cathy's cousin, Rachel, was driving with Cathy as a passenger in her car. The car was sucked under an eighteen-wheeler, and the two girls came out without a scratch. From the policemen at the scene and witnesses, we heard over and over that there was no way anyone should have survived that crash. Actually, the car looked much worse than the one from the crash that killed Cathy.

Of course, both Rachel and Cathy were emotionally scarred by this event. After that, the two made a pact that, if one of them should ever die, the one who died would send a message to the other through the computer. A few days later, Cathy wrote this poem, which I found in her room after her death:

Heaven's Gate

I thought I saw the gates open
But it wasn't for me
No, they weren't ready for me yet
My time will come
And when it does, I will be ready
I'm going to make my dreams come true
I'll do anything I want to do
I can't sit and watch my world go by
And when I finally walk through those gates
I will smile and say, "It was great!"
Hold on to the ones you love
They may be gone tomorrow
Don't grieve your life away for the ones you lost
You'll be back with them someday, tomorrow.

Cathy was never a religious person in any traditional sense. She usually chose only to attend church on holidays when she knew she'd get a new dress. But in the weeks before her death, she began talking to her co-workers about their views of God. Rachel recounted these stories for us, as the two girls worked together.

"I knew that she was becoming curious about spiritual things," Rachel recollected. "She knew I was a Christian. She asked Dana, who replied that she believed in God. I don't recall exactly what was said, but Dana and I shared that we both had been asked about God. We told Cathy what we believed, and that our beliefs did not really change who we are."

Although my children were reared in the Episcopal Church, I always expressed to them my belief that it was more important to be a good soul than a good churchgoer. When Cathy was young, she was a holy terror in church and I never knew what to expect from her during the service. I can recall one occasion when Cathy asked to excuse herself to use the restroom during a service. Our church was small and I had been attending this church since I was twelve years old, so I felt comfortable in letting my daughter go to the bathroom alone. While on her mission, she decided to call the emergency number, 911, from our priest's office. This caused quite a commotion, as we were in the middle of prayers when the sound of sirens roared from the church parking lot, breaking the silence. Since the emergency number had just been introduced to the community and our schools, Cathy was curious to know what would happen when dialing this magical number.

Cathy's life ended in the front yard of a church, and I had just finished decorating our own church for the Christmas Eve Service. Sometimes I wonder if her bad behavior during church was rooted somewhere in her psyche. Perhaps she knew a church was where her life would end.

Every morning I was accustomed to Cathy coming by my room to say "hello." One day she said something smart to me, and I retorted, "You're going to miss me when I'm gone." She stood there for a moment with tears filling her eyes, and slowly said, "How do you know I won't be the first to go?" This was only a couple days before she died. I still often cry when I recount this story, and I've heard many similar stories from others about the prescient things that their loved ones have done just before their deaths. I later learned that Cathy had told her cousin, "I feel like I'm living on borrowed time."

Cathy at St. Mark's Church

Her aura also changed in the week or so before her death. Although I admit that I cannot see auras, I could feel substantial differences in her beingness. There seemed to be a deep sadness about her. She was a vegetarian, so I worried about whether her dietary needs were being fully met. I just couldn't figure out why she seemed so different. In hindsight, I can see why these things must have been occurring.

Cathy's Cousins Eulogize Her

Of course, Cathy's memorial service is just a blur for me. Fortunately, her cousins later gave me copies of what they read at the funeral. I think it's important to include those stories here. They show a little more of what Cathy's life was about, speak a little more about how much she was loved.

When Brad, my sister Donna's older son, rose to speak, he talked about the time he proposed to his wife. Cathy had always told him that he would have to get her approval first before he could marry anyone, because as children he had proposed to Cathy first. He told stories of when they were young, how he would chase Cathy around. She would giggle and laugh, then tell him she was going to marry him one day.

Brad read his poem penned for this occasion at her service:

> *It's hard to know just what to say*
> *When one so young is taken away*
> *Far too soon she had to part*
> *Her memory forever engraved in my heart*
>
> *It seemed like I knew her for only awhile*
> *But it's all those memories that make me smile*
> *She was so beautiful, and oh, so rare*
> *What happened to her, it's just not fair*
>
> *All our love to Martha and Don*
> *For Cathy, whom we love, we must go on*
> *Those gone before will watch her with care*
> *Till the day comes when we join her up there*
>
> *Know that Cathy is watching from heaven above*
> *And with each ray of sunshine, she's sending us her love*

Cathy with Todd in 2001

Brad's brother, Todd, read this:

We have all been through the good and sad with Cathy. She was the kind of person who would only come to you when she was ready, like the Cat that she was. I remember when Cathy was sixteen years old, had her learner's permit, and wanted me to teach her to drive. She told me she had already been driving with her mom, so I let her get behind the wheel of my '87 Honda Accord.

We started down a straight and easy-to-drive road. Eventually, we came to an intersection with a stop sign. I told Cathy she could drive on if she wanted, so she began to turn right. She didn't turn sharply enough and ended up in the oncoming lane. Before I could say, "Take your time, everything's okay," she was feeling rushed by an oncoming car far down the road. She hit the gas, spun around 180 degrees and hit the stop sign we had just come through—in my precious Honda Accord! She was red, I was speechless and all she could say was, "I forgot to tell you, my mom hasn't taught me to turn yet."

I accepted that answer. I couldn't be mad at Cathy. Cathy is our baby, and that's probably why she got away with so much. I've known Cathy a very long time, and I have lots of memories of her. These memories are for me, to share with you, and this is only one small memory from the infinite number. It's important to share these memories to help complete the entire memory of Cathy.

We have all been through so much during this nightmare of Cathy's death. I feel as though things were once again rushed, and I never had a chance to say, "Slow down, everything's okay." I miss Cathy, and I don't understand God's decision, but I can't be mad at God. If Cathy is in a place of love, a place of warmth where she is truly happy, I can accept that.

Love, Todd Sloan

A friend, Mike, Cathy and Jamie in 2001

Jamie Sawyer, Rachel's brother, talked about once coming over to our house on a Saturday morning and wanting Cathy to go somewhere with him. Cathy was asleep and I warned Jamie that he would have to enter her room at his own risk. Cathy was not a morning person and did not like to be disturbed while sleeping. Jamie tiptoed into Cat's room and sat in a chair across from her while she was sleeping, wondering what he should do next. He picked up a wad of school paper on the floor and started rolling it into little spit balls and throwing it at Cathy's head. Jamie laughed as he described Cathy's reaction to what he was doing to her and how she first halfway opened one eye. Cathy just continued sleeping with one eye opened on Jamie and the other eye closed. Finally, her head popped up, and she resembled the character Linda Blair portrayed in *The Exorcist,* sending Jamie jumping for safety and out of harm's way. Jamie learned (the hard way) why I had cautioned him about entering Cathy's room while she was sleeping.

Each of us deals with grief in our own unique way, and Rachel was no different. A couple of months after Cathy's death, Rachel wrote this poem for her:

Marek and Cathy May 2001

Cathy and Rachel November 2001

Thought You Should Know

You should know that I don't understand the way I feel
This nightmare is all too surreal

And you should know why I just can't cry
It's because I can't comprehend this good-bye
I guess it just feels like you've moved far away
Like Okinawa, and I'll see you soon someday

You should know that the dolphins and eagles just won't do
And my world will never be the same here without you

You should know your mother cries every day and every night
And that it's so easy in the family now to start a fight
I just can't imagine this, no I cannot!
When I pass the hospital, it consumes all my thought

You should know when I come to Heaven's gate
That you'd better be waiting or heaven won't be so great

Of all these things that you should know
There's one most important before I go
I just thought that you should know
That I love you and miss you!
Just making sure ... that you know.

The poem's reference to dolphins and eagles speaks of the miniature copies of Cathy's urn with locks of her hair inside given to family members. While the urn which holds her ashes has dolphins on it, we also gave some family members tiny urns with eagles. It's easy to see why Rachel thought these small memorials could not come close to replacing her beloved cousin and friend.

Along with his cousins, Marek, Cathy's brother, eulogized her. He expressed the depth of his loss and how much he would miss his sister, the very best sister anyone could ever hope to have.

Cathy and Rachel
Best friends forever

George Anderson

Cathy's christening. Granddad Pierce is holding Cathy
and standing with Martha's father and mother

A few months after Cathy's death, we flew to Long Island to see George Anderson, a famous medium who was doing readings for members of Compassionate Friends. We had gone downstairs in the large hotel and were standing outside the hall where he was doing readings. I opened the door to the room to see what was going on. I thought I glimpsed Cathy in a white t-shirt and jeans, and she was smiling at me! A woman came out and hissed at us, "You're not supposed to be here! This is for Compassionate Friends!" We told her that we were with this group, and she hissed again, "Well, you're here at the wrong time." So we walked away and went back to our room.

I have a special necklace with three charms on it, and it was missing the next morning. The necklace was given to me by my niece Rachel and my nephews, Brad, Todd and Jamie, on my first Mother's Day without Cathy. I wear it all the time because it holds a heart charm that contains Cathy's hair and her picture. I have since added a ladybug charm, since ladybugs are Cathy's spiritual sign to me, and Cathy's godmother, Betty Kuhn, sent me a dolphin charm with two dolphins—mother and daughter. Betty knew that Cathy's urn had dolphins on it because she loved dolphins.

I feel I have Cathy with me almost all the time when wearing this necklace. I freak if I can't find it or think I have lost it. (I've found

myself hoping that nobody else sends me a charm to put on it, though.
The necklace is starting to look like real bling-bling.) So, of course, I
wanted to put on this necklace for our reading with George Anderson.
But the necklace had disappeared! I cried and prayed and carried on.
When we searched the room one last time, there it was! Don and I
were both puzzled at its reappearance, and this made us late for the
session with George Anderson, but I felt it was important to wear this
necklace. I'm glad I persisted in finding it.

When we sat down with him for the reading, it happened to be near
the date that would have been Cathy's twenty-first birthday. He began,
"I know that you feel now that you are carrying a heavy cross. But I
want you to know right now that you will all find resolve." I felt myself breathe deeply. This had indeed been a heavy cross.

As is usually the case when someone consults a mental medium,
George Anderson knew nothing about us. Anything he would tell us
during our session with him would be information that he was given
by his contacts on the Other Side or that he could figure out by watching us and seeing how we reacted to what he said.

George continued, "A male comes in, and a female follows, a
young female who is your daughter. She states that her grandfather is
with her." It's her great-grandfather Pierce who comes in; he was at
her christening and held her then. He gave us the lake property where
we had lived next to Ginny, and he was always close to Cathy.

"Your daughter draws close and embraces both people. She also
speaks of a tragic passing. It was very quick, with no suffering before
she passed. But she does speak of having injuries to the head. It feels
like something strikes her head. Once again, St. Joseph appears, signi-
fying a happy passing, in spite of the circumstances.... She definitely
assures you that she was gone in a moment. Gone in a flash. She says,
'Gone physically, but not forgotten spiritually. Alive spiritually, and
with you closely.' It may have killed you not to say good-bye then, but
she is here now to say, 'Hello'." This had quite an impact on me the
first time I heard it, and it moves me now when I listen to it again.

George Anderson continued, "She insists, too, that you recognize
that she had an accomplished life. 'A short one and an accomplished
one,' she says, especially to her Mom, who feels she was cheated out
of her life. But she wants you to remember that she wasn't. 'My
growth and life I can see and understand. You just want your daughter

back. Try to understand,' she says. It's a temporary situation, and she feels sorry for you, that you do feel like some of the other parents, temporarily abandoned. There is a triumph at the end, because there is

Crash site: Cathy was the passenger

a conclusion for it. The accident was no one's fault. I don't know how you feel, but that's what she says, and there must be a reason she says that. I'm confused. She did speak of another accident before this one, is that correct?"

"Yes," we replied.

George continued, "Okay, she does admit there was carelessness involved. Give credit where credit was due. The carelessness had no intention in it. You are her mom, and you will argue the point. But no one meant any harm. She has to say no one is at fault. Feeling someone is to blame doesn't make it any better. 'Think about it,' she says, 'and you tell me.' She says there was someone else who was involved in the accident who survived and adds, 'Isn't that always the way?' And there's no judgment in that, it was just her turn to pass, not the other person's. But it wasn't the other person's fault, she says. 'Just beware of holding any anger and blame, because who does this hurt? You? Or the person you think it's directed at?'

"As your daughter states, she has a tendency to tell it like it is, so why would it be any different now? She knows you'd like to wring somebody's neck, but that's not going to change anything that's occurred. She says, 'You didn't like that person to begin with, so it makes it a lot easier to blame, then, doesn't it?'

"I have to smile at the way she's saying this with such humor. 'It makes it a lot easier to blame, doesn't it?'"

The Copeland Family, 1996

This was true. The young woman who was driving the car, in which Cathy was killed, Bonnie, had stayed with us. I had actually put enve-

Cathy and her mother, Martha

lopes with money onto the Christmas tree for her. Although we had been nice to her, it was true that we didn't really appreciate her. It was amazing. Only Cathy would have picked up on this.

Back to George: "She says she still considers this person in friendship. 'She's not responsible for my death. You feel that in her carelessness, she murdered your daughter,' Cathy says, but she doesn't see it that way. 'Even if I think they're wrong,' she says, 'you have a right to your feelings. But I'm telling you the way I see it.' She hopes by sharing this with you that you might see things a little differently. She says both of you had no use for the person, but you might have at least been more flexible. 'You had brick walls,' she says. That's why she addresses this now; her friend was special to her."

George's reading continued, "'Her heart is in the right place, and this was part of her journey,' she says. She said to you, as her mom, were a little protective. When mothering her, you sometimes smothered her. You could knock heads." At this, George made catfight sounds and motions.

"But you had a unique, loving friendship and you understood each other, even when you couldn't see eye-to-eye. As much as you worry about her, she's just trying to help you understand the situation and bring you into a more understanding state. 'You thought it's only a matter of time until this person messes up my daughter,' she says, 'But stop stirring the pot!' But she says this, too, to her Dad, that she knows you suffer in silence about this."

Turning to Don, George continued, "She says to me she has more than one dad. But she wants to have you know that you are her 'Dad of the Heart.' When she refers to you as Dad, she explains it to me. It's kind of funny. She does call out to her own dad. She says there's a lack of communication there, but she says, 'What else is new?' It seems there never was a good relationship, but she does call out to him. He's still her dad. And she certainly does thank you, as her second father, for being so supportive to her mom."

"Cathy does admit that, although she was smart, she was also a little naïve. Could be a little on the trusting side," George said. This was certainly true. At one point, she had decided to move out and get her own apartment. We had given her $5,000 that was part of the settlement from when the dog attacked her. It should have lasted at least a few months, but Cathy tended to be generous and not always discriminating and she and her friends blew all of it in three weeks.

Toward the end of the interview, George said, "She's trying to say 'Hello to Rachelle.' Do you know a Rachelle?" I later realized that she was greeting Rachel, who was her favorite cousin, and who first heard from Cathy on the computer.

George went on, "She admits that at times she could be a kind of rebellious little creature. You'll be happy to know she's calmed down a little bit, that she sees things in a different light. Both of you sometimes had your hands full with her, and you would now give anything to have another five minutes of that with her. She says the feeling is there always now, because she is here with you. You've had many signs, evidence that she is close. And again, she says that she is always there. You worry about her, but she's the last person you should worry about.

"'If she were to go to Mongolia, she'd find her way back,' she says. Again, she says that grandparents are with her (on the Other Side), but she's still very uniquely and independently on her own. She embraces all of those who love her. She says not to be afraid for her, that she's all right. And do evaluate what she's said, to take the bitterness out of your hearts. With that, she says she steps aside now, because there's someone else who wants to talk."

When we went for this reading, we were still in a state of shock from Cathy's death. I think this state of shock lasts for at least a year or two when someone close dies. And now that the grief is a little better, a little less raw, we can look at this information again. I'm now getting a lot more from this reading than I was unable to pick up the first time around, or even months afterward.

Indeed, my distress with Bonnie was a big factor after the accident. In order to take some of the stinging grief away, I did focus too much on the anger I felt toward her as the driver of the car in which Cathy was killed. Truly, these words, which Cathy was able to convey to me through George Anderson, helped to assuage my rage considerably. From that point on, I was able to reassess why I had been directing so much anger at someone who had only been a party to this tragedy. I knew that there had been no ill intent. I felt that Cathy wanted me to overcome quickly so I could focus on something else. When I began to let go of the anger, I became able to contact Cathy more easily. It was as if my anger had formed a barrier that didn't allow Cathy in.

Through his writing and his speaking, George Anderson continually reminds us that souls communicate with us here on Earth for many reasons, primarily because they want to. In his book, *Walking in the Garden of Souls*, he says, "For them it is a joy to help our spiritual growth on earth, and they are in the hereafter working as our 'guardian angels' so that we can come to the same reward in the hereafter when our time on earth is done." These words and George's reading for us still give me considerable comfort.

Walking in the Garden of Souls, www.georgeanderson.com/books.htm

First Contact

Cathy had been dead for five months. It had been excruciating, more difficult for all of us than we could ever have imagined. One night Rachel got up during the night, unable to sleep. On the Internet she found something about Electronic Voice Phenomena or EVP. With new hope, she tried and tried to get something through the computer. Frustrated, she started crying and kicking things around in her room. She yelled, "Cat, you promised me you'd come back. You promised, and now I'm alone." With tear-filled eyes, Rachel sat down at her computer to try one more time.

"I'm still here" came through in a very faint voice, followed by, *"How do you know they can hear?"* in a male voice. Then came Cathy's sigh, so typical of what I remember throughout her life. When I'd ask her to clean her room, I'd always hear that sigh. Yes, this was certainly Cathy.

My First Recorded Message

After Cathy's first accident with Rachel, and perhaps even before that, Cathy seemed more interested in topics concerning death and the after-life. When I went through her room following her fatal accident, I found several books pertaining to the topic, including some on EVP. For me, this may be part of the reason why she has been adept in communicating with us, and why she seems to be a "ringleader" on the Other Side.

After Rachel heard from Cathy, I very much wanted to contact her myself. Day after day I sat at my computer and tried. My husband, Don, reminded me that some days I'd be at my computer, still in my nightgown, when he left for work. And I'd be sitting there in my nightgown when he arrived back home in the evening.

At one point, I became so frustrated that I asked the silence sur-rounding my computer, "Why can Rachel reach you but I cannot?" When I played it back, there was Cathy's voice … at last, *"Mama, I'm right here."*

Thrilled, I called members of my family over to hear the tape. But when they arrived, the message had disappeared. They looked at me like I was ready for the funny farm. When they all left, I got really de-pressed. I just sat and cried. It was as if I had lost her all over again. That night before falling asleep, I prayed that she would help me find her voice recording. I wanted to assure myself and my worried family that I was not going crazy.

Around 4:00 A.M., I was awakened by Cathy's voice in my mind saying, *"Mom, you've got to try again."* Still feeling sad and ex-hausted from crying, I silently responded, "Go away and leave me alone." I heard Cathy's soft response, *"You do not need to use the computer. You can hear me in your head."*

The next morning when I opened the file, I found her recording on the computer. My husband and family members were then able to hear it. Don was so thrilled about all of this that he purchased an audio management program for the computer and surround-sound speakers, just to make sure I'd get the best quality of any messages received.

The Family Gathers

Family Gathering: (clockwise) Martha's mother and father, Todd, Jamie, Donna, Brad, Don, Ginny and Cathy holding Muffin

I pick up my Sony digital recorder. This is not the recorder I usually use to contact Cathy. I've found that it helps to use just one or two machines for each person I want to contact, and a Panasonic IC recorder is "Cathy's recorder." But today I want to record the family's stories, so the Sony, which has a good track record, will do the trick. I turn it on and hear my own voice saying to Cathy, "I wish you were here. I know you're here, but I can't see you. I wish we could talk now, Cat." Then I sit and listen to three or four minutes of silence. I realize I've spent a lot of time lately just sitting and listening. It comforts me in many ways.

Perhaps this is insane (according to others' definitions of sanity). But anyone who has lost a child already knows how it feels to stand on the brink of insanity. Grief this deep sends you to that edge and finding one's way back from the brink is difficult and agonizing work. And who's to say which of us has fallen into the abyss and who has managed to draw themselves back from the edge?

Now my family is arriving to tell stories for this book. We've all gathered in the family room with a half dozen dogs. It's bittersweet, this remembering Cathy. We begin to speak, sometimes in turn, sometimes right over each other, and it's not long before everyone, even my dad, is in tears. Here are the stories from my beloved family members, told in their own words:

Fateful Night

Donna tells this story:

It was Christmastime, and I was at the church with Martha to do the decorations for the Christmas pageant that night. We were having a good time talking about the dinner we were going to have, and we stopped to get a ham. I stood in line for the ham, and Martha went over to get decorations. She came back, and I heard her yelling something. I thought she said that she had wrecked my car. But I was standing in line for my ham, so I decided that I couldn't do anything about the car at the moment. I was just going to continue to stand in line! I'd rather have the ham than the car. Martha persisted, screaming and yelling, and people started to push me out the door. Then I heard, "Cathy has been in a wreck!" All I could think was, "Oh, my gosh! What if she's broken a leg or hurt her hand? How will we get her up and down the stairs? How will we deal with the cast?"

As we drove toward the hospital, all I can remember is these thoughts about dealing with the aftermath of the accident. Beyond these thoughts, I seemed hypnotized by the windshield wipers going back and forth, plus all the traffic around us. Suddenly, Martha said, "She's dead." I said, "That's not true, Martha, don't say that." And Martha said, "I know it. She's dead."

When we got to the hospital, it was a long ordeal. Chuck Girardeau, the preacher, came to sit with us. Thank goodness he was there. Finally the doctors found us, all sitting around. I thought they were going to say, "Well, she's going to be in traction and you're going to have to do this and that." But instead they said the dreaded words, "Well, we did everything we could..." We all looked up in surprise, like "What are you saying?" They repeated, "We did everything we could, but she's gone." We sat there stunned, and someone on the staff said, "Is there anything we can do for you?" I remember Martha said, "Yeah, bring her back."

Then they let us go into the examination room, and there she was, like she was sleeping. Martha still talks about her first thoughts as we walked into the room, "Oh, Cathy, you've left me with this horrible dog, and I don't know what to do with it! I don't understand this dog!" She talked non-stop to Cathy from the minute we walked in the door. Finally, a trauma team volunteer came in and said something about being with the body. Martha exclaimed, "The body! This is not just a body! This is my daughter, not a body!" The volunteer started preaching about acceptance, like she was going to force us through the steps of grief in five minutes. We were stunned by

Cathy's dog, Doja

such insensitivity by a medical professional. I thought Martha was going to hit the volunteer, and she is less than five feet tall! With this exchange, the reality of her loss hit hard, and her grief just overwhelmed her.

Rainbows

Donna, who travels extensively for her work, tells another story:

> I can always feel Cathy close to me while traveling on airplanes. Recently I had not felt Cathy around for awhile. Shortly after I noticed this, I was traveling home on a plane, and I closed my eyes, asking for a sign from Cathy. Opening my eyes, I looked out of the window of the plane and saw a small rainbow. This rainbow did not cover the sky—it was merely there in front of my window for just a few seconds. I got the sign I was looking for! So I thanked Cathy.

Ginny's Medication

Ginny remembers this:

> I have very high blood pressure, and I'm on medication for it. Some time after Cathy was killed, everybody was in turmoil, including me. Because I had to work that night at the hospital, I

went to bed early, forgetting to take my medication. I had taken aspirin because I had a bad headache, and as I was dropping off to sleep, I heard Cathy's voice in my head, with her usual touch of playfulness, "Don't forget your medication." Apparently I had dreamt she was there. She came to me just like we were having a conversation, and I awoke and remembered to take it. Either this was my subconscious awakening me, or it was Cathy. I don't care which it was, because it saved me.

Cathy Dreams

Rachel tells these stories:

After the first accident in my car, we made a pact that if anything happened to one of us, we would come back and contact the other. We hadn't really said how we were going to contact each other. We had been talking, kind of goofing around about it, and Cathy said, "Yeah, I'm going to come through your computer and just write my name, Cat-Cat-Cat-Cat-Cat-Cat, all over the screen. You'll never forget me!" I said, "Okay, you can haunt me." I did notice that my computer would crash more often after Cathy died. There seemed to be a ghost in the machine.

I've never had a dream where I see her dead. Some people, when they've had a loved one die, have dreams where they see the person in a coffin. That has never occurred for me. I've only had dreams about me visiting her. One dream was funny because I was so emotional. It felt like heaven to me, all grassy and nature-like. All these young women were sitting in a circle. I saw Cathy and walked up to her, giving her hugs and kisses, "I'm so happy to see you again!" And the other girls were laughing at me, saying "Why are you doing that?" And I just looked at them and said, "Because I love her so much." It was really amazing to me, because I could feel her right there, in the flesh. It was like being with her again. I remembered clear through my body what it was like to hug her. I was just thoroughly enjoying myself, and she said, "Well, you should come more often." And I thought I might, because it was really fun to be with her again.

I have dreams about Cathy a lot. I think I used to remember a lot more when I awoke. Some of the memories are fading now. I can only remember her face; I have a harder time knowing what being with her was about. And the dreams of her have dropped off. Recently I've been having more nightmares. But if I want to see her again, I'll repeat her name in my mind as I'm going to sleep, so that we can meet in my dreams.

Cremation

Now it's my turn to talk about a couple of things, which have been amazing and difficult for us all:

"Cool Cat" on the Lake: Cathy holding Tiger, Hida, Todd, Donna

I didn't want to cremate Cathy's body. After the accident, she just looked so perfect, so beautiful. I just couldn't stand the thought of her burning. She had always been "Cool Cat," and I couldn't imagine her being on fire. But she had been insistent about it in the months before her death. She told me that she didn't want to rot in the ground and be eaten by worms. So we did it.

I remember going to shop for urns. We finally settled on one with dolphins since Cathy had loved them so much. It was stunning to me that her birth father insisted upon having some of the ashes. He had not done much to maintain a good relationship with Cathy. The last time she had gone to visit him, he would not even let her stay at his house. She cried all the way home. Ginny said we should just scoop some ashes out of the fireplace to give to him, that he wouldn't know the difference. We laughed at that, but we shared Cathy's ashes with him. It was just another difficult part of a truly awful time.

Donna adds:

Right after Cathy died, we went on a trip we'd planned to the Cayman Islands. After we returned, I took my film to have it developed, and when I went to pick up the pictures, the guy said, "I think some of the pictures on here were old." I started leafing through them … islands … islands … islands. Then all of a sudden, there were pictures of Cathy in a coffin. I don't remember taking those pictures, and I don't know who would have gotten hold of my camera. But there were five pictures of Cathy in a coffin! It was such a jolt to see that image in the midst of the vacation pictures, but later we found real comfort in having those last pictures of Cathy.

More Funeral Pictures

I have had two experiences of having Cathy's funeral pictures pop up unexpectedly on my computer screen. Because of my strong belief in the afterlife, I had my nephews take photos with digital cameras of Cathy in her coffin during our private family viewing. It was my hope to capture Cathy's spirit in these photos, because I knew she was around us.

Months passed by and I had forgotten about the photos until sitting at my computer. My phone rang and it was the clerk at the courthouse notifying me of the upcoming trial date for Bonnie, the girl responsible for Cathy's death. As soon as I placed the phone up to my ear to answer, the computer screen was covered with the funeral pictures of Cathy in her coffin. Needless to say, I let out a blood-curdling scream and frightened the poor court clerk on the line. After this incident my husband intended to remove the funeral pictures from my computer so this would never happen again.

Three weeks before Cathy's graduation from high school, she dropped out unexpectedly from school. I was furious with her because she was so close to the end and she knew how important completing school was to me. We had already purchased her graduation attire and had promised her a trip for two anywhere in the world as her graduation gift. Eventually, Cathy did go back to school and passed the exam to receive her GED certificate but was killed before she was able to pick it up. Because I knew it mattered to Cathy, I wanted this certificate to frame and place in her room. While waiting for a return phone call from the Georgia Department of Education to see what documents were required to release the GED certificate to me, my phone rang. While a clerk from the Georgia Department of Education was informing me that Cathy's death certificate was the only requirement, the photos of Cathy in her coffin reappeared on my computer screen. Al-

Martha, Ginny and Donna beside Cathy's coffin

though this was extremely upsetting, I managed to restrain another blood-curdling scream.

Even now I am still puzzled as to what message (if any) Donna and I were meant to receive from those funeral photos.

Cell Phone Messages

Soon after her death, I decided to take Cathy's phone down to the phone company to see if I could retrieve the messages from it. I was curious about what might have been happening just before she died. At the phone store, someone told me to wait in a small, private office,

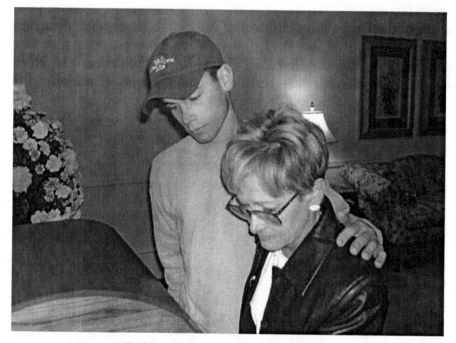

Todd and Martha beside Cathy's coffin

telling me that it might take fifteen to twenty minutes to retrieve messages. I sat down with the phone. Suddenly, it began to ring! This was strange, because service had already been cut off. I just sat there staring at it, and then finally decided to pick up. There was nothing but static, white noise at the other end. Then I heard a young female voice say, "I know Cathy." Still in shock, I'm guessing I sat there listening to it for awhile before I hung up.

When the phone guy came out to tell me about the messages, I told him what had happened. He grinned, and I asked him if he could trace the call. He gave it a try, but the number that showed up on Cathy's cell phone was not traceable.

Later, after I had begun regularly to record EVP with the Recording Circle - Bridge to the Afterlife group, I remembered the cell phone

Cathy with Shishi

incident when hearing the EVP voice of Judy Quillen's daughter Jamie. My eyes widened as I realized that this sounded very much like the voice on Cathy's cell phone!

Visitations with Grandma

My mother tells these stories about Cathy:

> One day I am sitting on the sofa in the living room, drifting off, watching television. All of a sudden, I see a bright, bright outline of Cathy. The colors are dramatic, more beautiful than anything I've ever seen. There is a brilliant light around her, and she is reaching out for me. Cathy's face is absolutely radiant. She looks so happy. I am jolted awake, and I notice my hands are in the air, reaching toward her.
>
> This visit isn't all that strange to me. Years ago, I happened to look down while I was working in the kitchen. Shishi was a dog Martha had gotten years ago when they were living in Okinawa,

Japan. A big, fluffy dog with large, round, human-looking eyes, Shishi had died a month before Cathy, and she's been heard in EVP with Cathy. Anyway, here's Shishi right in front of me! There was sort of a grayish radiance around her as she stood there in my house. She looked quizzical, like she wanted to communicate something to me, and wondered why she couldn't. I decided to just stand there and watch her until she was gone. It took awhile, and she did begin to fade. I watched until she was completely gone.

In the summer before she died, Cathy was at my house, sitting on the same couch where she appeared to me later. We were talking, and the subject of death came up. "I want to be cremated," she said. "I don't want to be buried." I argued with her, but she said, "I don't want bugs and worms crawling all over me. I want to be cremated."

Sometime after Cathy's death, we were upstairs in Martha's office. Martha and Ginny were there with me, along with their dad, and I was trying for the first time to get Cathy to speak through the computer. I said, "Cathy, are you being good?" And I was stunned to hear my brother's voice. He had died on September 15, 1967, and right there in the room, his unmistakable voice boomed, *"You're damned right she is!"*

My mother's brother, Marcus James, nicknamed M.G., was a real character, or perhaps by some, was considered a nutcase. He loved to play tricks on people and had to be the center of attention. However, M.G. also had a very sadistic side to him. I remember how he used to pull my baby dolls' heads off and hold them up high so I couldn't reach them, teasing me as he laughed. My dolls were like real babies to me and this used to really upset me and make me cry.

(My father told me a story about a time when M.G. painted my father's back with green paint while he was asleep on a blanket at the beach. Despite all the pranks, M.G. was my father's best friend, and they shared a close bond. It wasn't a surprise to me that, during my mother's first attempt to reach Cathy, M.G. came through instead. I am sure M.G. got a real thrill out of seeing my dad jump to his feet when his voice came through my speakers.)

My mother continues her stories:

> My brother, M.G., was fourteen months older than I, and we were always close.
>
> When he died, my nephew took me to the funeral home, but he didn't want to go in, so I went in alone to say goodbye. I felt a calm feeling of warmth and light surrounding me during my entire visit. Then I heard a voice say, "Blessed are they that mourn, for they shall be comforted." Angels? Holy Ghost? Perhaps it was my mother. Because before her death, she had told me that she would come through to me since I have the psychic gift her mother had. Maybe this was her way from the Other Side of comforting me in my grief.
>
> I recall sitting out in the garage, shooting the breeze with M.G. a week before he died. He had said, "If you go first, come back and tell me what it's like, and I'll do the same if I go first." Of course, I was very upset. When my brother died, an old, broken music box started playing again. Years ago one night my husband and I were in bed. We had an old television set with rabbit ears covered in tin foil. I said, "M.G., if you're in this room, make the tin foil fall off." Nothing happened. But the next night it did fall off. Soon after, Donald, my husband (Cathy's grandpa), had a dream and saw M.G. reaching for him much like Cathy had been reaching for me. Later he told me that M.G. had said, "Come on, Red." (This was my husband's nickname due to his head full of red hair.) Donald said he saw M.G. hovering over him, and he felt himself begin to rise up out of his body. He stopped it all by saying, "I'm not going there. No thanks."
>
> Some time afterward my mother died. I was in the kitchen preparing dinner for Thanksgiving. I heard a voice say, "Sallie!" I stopped in the kitchen and walked into the hall, hearing "Sallie!" again. I pulled down the stairs and began messing in the attic, I was so nervous. "Sallie!" The telephone rang. It was Dr. Vernon Cofer in Norfolk calling, "I hate to tell you, but your father just passed away." The news was difficult, but not surprising. I had known something had happened. My mother had already told me.

[My Grandmother James was a very spiritual woman and used to tell me stories about Edgar Cayce who was one of the most renowned psychic healers of the time. Edgar Cayce's son, Hugh Lynn Cayce, had attended my grandfather's business school. My grandmother once said that Edgar Cayce would pay for his son's tuition from out of an old sock he carried in his pants.]

My mother continues:

> Cathy was special. I felt she had been passed down my grandmother's gift, too; but she was indeed her own person, and didn't want to be told what to do by anyone. She was a beautiful person, a lovely girl. She was a great lover of animals. She liked them and trusted them even more than people.
>
> Sometime in the summer before she died, she stayed overnight. She awoke right around lunchtime. "Let me fix you a grilled cheese," I said. Cathy was vegetarian, and this was a favorite meal. I fixed her one, then another. She ate those along with a soda. "Grandma, you make the best grilled cheese." She was sitting around at the lake house in her little shorts, and somehow we started talking about death. "I'd never be buried," she said. I smiled and said, "I don't want to be burned, although I might be when I get where I'm going." We laughed.

Cat Dreams

Since we first began communicating with Cathy, it seems that her presence is felt around us more and more. Many family members tell stories now about Cathy having appeared to them in dreams or otherwise communicating with them. It is always balm to my soul to collect these stories from those I love. My sister Ginny tells these stories:

> Last night I dreamed I was talking to Cat. We sat and talked about things, some I can't remember. We talked about the garden that her mom and I are working on, and she said that she likes it, and that it helps her mom. At one point she said, "Yeah, I'm worried about my mom," but didn't explain why. As we talked, she suddenly said, 'Oh, Aunt Ginny! Somebody just broke your new mailbox." I told her that I had actually just fixed my mailbox that the last one had been broken, but I had just bought and installed a new one with a decorative colonial finial on top of it.

"Rachel and I are proud of the new installation," I told her, "The old one is gone."

She looked at me in the dream and sharply said, "No." Then she somehow showed me a picture of a car with two boys and a baseball bat breaking my new mailbox. Now we were both standing in my driveway, still in the dream, and Cathy said, "Don't worry, it can be fixed." I remember Cathy was wearing jeans with a T-shirt and an unzipped gray hooded jacket.

When I awoke, I kind of shook my head, thinking it was a stupid dream. I took out my garbage for pick-up, and there was my broken mailbox! Apparently someone had hit the top with a baseball bat and knocked off the finial. Just like Cathy had told me, I was able to fit the piece back again.

I'll admit to being a skeptic about most things, so I still

Cathy at the lake

thought all this was mere chance. I went into my bathroom to get ready for the day, still bugged about this entire event. As I was about to spray my hair, a ladybug (Cathy's spiritual sign) walked across the mirror, stopping right in front of me. I wanted to capture the ladybug and take it outside. But when I turned around, it was gone.

Cathy's Foot

My sister Donna tells this story about events which unfolded in the days after Cathy's death:

I'll never forget that night. It was just after midnight, early in the morning of Christmas Eve. Martha, her husband, Don, and I were walking across the hospital parking lot—all of us in a daze. Cathy was dead. The night air was crisp and cold, and I was shivering. I looked down and noticed that Don was carrying a small, clear plastic bag in his hand. Taking a closer look, I noticed the bag held Cathy's tennis shoes and socks. I felt as though I had been punched hard in the stomach, that all that we had left of our Cathy was in that small plastic bag. The reality of it was overwhelming.

Later, in the early morning hours of Christmas Eve, I tried to get a couple hours of sleep, but could not. My mind was racing—we had to make funeral arrangements early, because the funeral home closed at noon on Christmas Eve. What about Christmas? What about the gifts I had planned to buy at the last minute? I worried about everything, even Christmas, even when I knew we would no longer be celebrating. I could feel my heart pounding as I lay there. But in the midst of all the tossing and turning, I suddenly felt Cathy's presence in the room. I couldn't see her, but I could feel her all around me. It was so strong that I asked out loud, "Are you all right?" She answered very briefly but very clearly, ***"My foot hurts."***

Later at the funeral home, I asked the funeral director if Cathy's feet looked like they had been injured in the accident. He said he did not notice any injuries. I felt much better, because I hated to think that she might still feel any pain on the Other Side.

About six months later, Martha learned that there was going to be a psychic fair in the neighboring town. I had never visited a psychic before, but she and our other sister Ginny wanted me to go along, and I have to admit I was a little curious. So I decided to go along with them.

The psychic fair was teeming with mediums from all over the country. I looked over the list of psychics and after studying their credentials, selected two that I wanted to visit. My sisters selected different psychics so we'd make sure the psychics we met with did not "pick up" information from one of us to use on the next.

My first psychic encounter was just as I had imagined it would be—mostly generalities. Of course, a woman my age would most likely have a deceased grandparent. And of course, someday I was going to get a lot of money. (To this, I thought, "Sure, of course not!") So I was pretty convinced it was all just hokey.

My second encounter, however, left me a little less skeptical. I met with a slender, young, rather ordinary-looking man. I really didn't expect too many surprises from him. He asked me if I wanted to know about anyone in particular. I asked, "How is Cathy?" He thought for a minute and said, "She's fine. At first she had some problems, something about her leg or foot hurting, but she's fine now."

Nanny's Funeral

At that psychic fair, despite the agreement I had made with my sisters to use different psychics for reading, I requested a reading from the same medium that told Donna about Cathy's foot hurting. His name was Jason Lewis and he came from Kentucky. He told me that Cathy was thanking me for honoring someone in the family. Jason said that she was saying that I would be traveling by plane this summer, and presenting a speech to honor this person.

In early June, which would have been Cathy's grandmother's

Nanny, Martha's mother, Marek and Cathy

ninety-first birthday, our beloved Nanny became very ill. I received an EVP from Cathy saying, *"Mom, Nanny's coming."* Naturally, I immediately telephoned Nanny. She had just recently moved from her home into an assistant care home with her own apartment. Possessing a wonderful, warm personality, Nanny had already made several new friends in the complex. She was always full of energy and had just recently given up driving and even though she was elderly, she was one of those people you just could never imagine dying. Nanny reminded me of a landmark and even though I was no longer in the Amiss family, we had remained close. The night I called Nanny she told me that the doctor told her she was too sick to start her new volunteer job at the hospital. Her old heart was finally giving out and she needed to rest. Nanny was crying as she told me this, and then admitted that she was not ready to die, that she had too many things she wanted to accomplish first. We talked about Cathy, and I told Nanny that I had been receiving messages from Cathy from the Other Side and she seemed to be happy. I told Nanny that if she had to go, not to be afraid, that Cathy would be waiting for her, along with the rest of her family in spirit.

Nanny told me, "You know, Martha, Cathy was always my favorite." She recollected a time while driving when Cathy was still little, in the backseat of her car and having an automobile accident. (Nanny had several!) Smoke filled the inside of the vehicle. Just as Nanny was about to ask Cathy if she was alright, she heard a little voice chiming, "Uhhh-Ohoooo …better get MAACO!" Nanny said that despite everything, she had to laugh.

Before hanging up, I told Nanny I loved her and she said the same to me. The next day, I received a call from a family member, Jackie Dickerson, informing me that Nanny had died and inviting me to speak at her funeral.

I really wasn't sure if I could do this. Yet I remembered what the medium, Jason, had told me Cathy had said, that she was thanking me for honoring someone in the family. Clearly, this someone was Nanny, and I knew this was the first funeral since Cathy's death that I would be attending. Indeed, Nanny was someone who had been special in my life.

My son, Marek, along with my friends, Irene Matzgannis and Carolyn Phaup, attended the funeral with me. The service was held at

Nanny's church, Hampton Baptist Church in Hampton, Virginia, where she had sung in the choir for many years. Her former minister, Chester Brown, commented on how crowded the church was for someone of her age. Irene had cautioned me that my nerves could not handle this yet and begged me not to give a speech. I had prepared Marek to take over for me if necessary, but when my time came, I left the pew and walked to the lectern. Facing the congregation, I heard these words boom from my mouth, as if I had no control of what was being said:

> After losing my daughter Catherine Amiss on December 23, 2001, a grief therapist told me that every family has one person that is the "glue" for the rest of the family.
>
> Kathy Amiss, or as we called her, "Nanny," was the "Super-glue" for this family.
>
> Both Cathy and Nanny's lives, one cut short and one long, had a tremendous impact on so many of us.
>
> This is why today we are feeling the emotions of sadness and joy. A hole has been left in our souls that can never again be filled in this lifetime. At the same time, I take great comfort in knowing that Cathy and Nanny will be waiting for me on the Other Side.
>
> I love you both.

Feeling the presence of Nanny on one side of me and Cathy on the other gave me the courage to go through with the eulogy. Irene later told me that she and Carolyn looked over at each other with shocked expressions while I was speaking. She commented, "Martha, it was so perfect. It didn't even sound like your voice coming out of your mouth."

Returning to Irene's house after the funeral, we were all standing in her kitchen, and all at once, our mouths dropped opened as this huge ladybug walked across the window. Irene told me that she had never before seen a ladybug in her house. I knew Cathy and Nanny were thanking me.

Thanks to my Church

My family has long attended church together at St. Mary and St. Martha of Bethany Episcopal Church in Buford, Georgia. But after Cathy's death, I just found it too difficult to face many of the questions people had for me. Eventually, I wrote this letter to my church family:

Although I have not been attending church since my daughter Cathy's death, my family keeps me well posted on what is going on, telling me of your support for my well-being. Thank you so much for everything you have done for my family, Cathy and me. This tragic time would have been impossible to bear if it was not for the loving support of my family and my church friends.

Some say change is good; somehow my soul disagrees. When we remember the year 2001, we will never forget all the loss. Cathy's auto accident on December 23, 2001, made me redefine who I am. My soul feels like it's in limbo, somewhere between the living and the dead. The loss of a child is a most terrible thing, for children are God's most precious gift to us. The Grinch not only stole my Christmas, he stole my joy for living. Every holiday and special occasion is now just a sad reminder of the gift I once had. How should I answer when someone asks me how many children I have? Should I reply, "One" or "Two"? It's just so confusing! This once alive and noisy house has now become a silent, sad and grieving house.

A small ladybug was tattooed on Cathy's stomach. Now it seems that ladybugs are invading my house—and also the church. I felt Cathy would have been pleased at the story my sisters told me:

During a service, Lloyd, our assistant priest, had to stop two little boys from swishing ladybugs around. It's no surprise they would show up at our church! My family and I purchase ladybug things; I now have quite a collection of them at my house.

The lyrics from Cathy's favorite song seem to fit me well. I listen to Nelly Furtado's voice singing, "I'm like a bird … I only fly away … I don't know where my soul is…." Someday I hope to return to my church and all my faithful, caring friends. Thank you again for all your caring. Thank you, too, to those who donated the Easter flowers in memory of Cathy. Please understand why I do not return phone calls or why I've been unable to express my gratitude in person for all you have done. Every phone call, note or expression of loving support does not go unnoticed or unappreciated. Day after day it gives me the strength to crawl out of bed and make sure all of Cathy's animals have been fed.

Every time you see a ladybug, please send a prayer to my Cathy in heaven. May peace be with you.

Very sincerely yours,
Martha Copeland, Cathy's Mom

Cathy Still Watches Over
Our Animals!

Muffin, Cathy at twelve and Shishi

Several weeks ago my sister Ginny and I were doing a recording session. While I was out of the room, she picked up my Cathy's voice saying, *"Mama, I have Muffin."* This was followed by the sound of a dog. Muffin was her dog of seventeen years, who died shortly after Cathy.

Yesterday October 7, 2002, I was on the computer and received another message from Cathy saying, "I can't find Fluffy." Fluffy was a cat we had about fifteen years ago. We were being transferred overseas, and we planned to take him with us. However, I accidentally hit Fluffy with the car just before our departure date, so he was unable to make the long journey. We left him with a loving family and tearfully said goodbye. Fortunately, Fluffy survived, recovered and lived an active life.

Many of my meditations and dreams are with Cathy. Often we are walking in a meadow surrounded by our many animals. Some are animals we've had as a family; some are animals I had loved as a

Martha's brother, Chip, holding Fluffy

child. Not realizing it until after her last message, it suddenly dawned on me that I had never seen Fluffy during those dreams and meditations.

When I tried to save the recording which said Cathy couldn't find Fluffy, the computer crashed. I thought I had lost it. Disappointed and sad, I decided to get out of the house for a couple of hours.

Upon returning, I noticed Cathy's bedroom door ajar. This was unusual; this door is always closed. Entering her room, I noticed a piece of paper on the floor in front of the doorway. A note in Cathy's handwriting read, "I smile because I love U, I love U because U care (then a picture of a smiley face) U care to make me happy, & always be there!" This piece of paper seemed to be Cathy's way of reassuring me that she would always be with me.

Marek holding Fluffy, Cathy holding Penny

Checking around with family members and friends of Cathy, I found that no one else had been in my house. Later my niece, Rachel, was anxious to see the note for herself, so she dropped by. She recalled that Cathy had written the note a while back, but she had placed it inside a notebook. To this day I don't know why Cathy's door was open on that day and the note left on the floor. It remains a mystery!

At the same time, this note seemed to answer an ongoing question. "What if I go to the Other Side," I'd wonder, "only to find that Cathy has already gone to another level? What would become of our mother and daughter relationship that I treasured?" Receiving this note was reassurance that our relationship of love would continue.

Cathy's ability to interact with animals has shown up in a variety of ways. One day I was snapping green beans for Thanksgiving dinner the next day. Donna dropped by to ask if I wanted to go shopping. It doesn't take much to twist my arm in that direction, so I dropped the task and we took off for the mall. I left the bowl of green beans on the sofa in the den. I forgot that Cathy's dog, Doja, was in the house, too.

When I returned home, my den was covered with chewed-up green beans. This ornery dog had also decided to transplant some of my

Cathy with (left to right) Pookie, Winnie, Penny, Muffin and Shishi in 1998

houseplants—without consideration of finding a new pot for them! Also, the fresh flowers on the table got added to the mess. Then I noticed that my voice-activated recorder had been left running on the kitchen table. I flipped it off, and once I recovered from the shock of the mess, I decided to listen to it. There was Cathy's voice, sharply saying, *"Doja, NO!"* (This EVP can be heard by going to the www.aaevp.com website.) I wonder if this kept him from doing any further damage!

The day after Thanksgiving, I awoke and did some recording. I kept getting Cathy's voice saying, ***"Penny... Penny..."*** Penny was the name of one of my parents' dogs, and my mother called later that day to let us know that my dad was taking Penny to the vet because she was sick. Penny was nineteen years old and had to be put down that day. I wondered whether Cathy had seen Penny there with all the animals who join us in the meadow.

Elaney

Cathy with her "Rats" and Rachel

After Cathy's death, my sister Ginny took Cathy's rat, Elaney. I was terrified of it! Ginny has since become very fond of the creature. She feeds it snacks and lets it run around her room every day. She even gives it a kiss before going to work!

After expressing my disgust in hearing this, Ginny's reply to me was, "Some people kiss husbands, I kiss my rat …you tell me which is worse?"

The other day, Ginny was using her daughter, Rachel's, computer. Rachel happened to be stretched on her bed, studying for an exam. Ginny decided to attempt to record EVP and asked for Cathy. When Ginny played back her recording using Audition, both she and Rachel heard Cathy singing! Rachel jumped up and said, "That's Cathy singing!" They heard, *"Elaney, Elaney, I miss my rat, Elaney!"* Ginny had been holding Elaney and petting her before she began the recording.

Ginny saved the message on her IC recorder. She came to my house to share with me the recording of Cathy. We played back the recording, but Cathy's voice was not heard on the recorder. Cathy must have come through only during the time Ginny had her recorder hooked up to the computer. Unfortunately, Ginny failed to save that recording on her computer!

Ginny was disappointed about this, but I told her that we would hear from Cathy again. I feel Cathy might be preparing Ginny for Elaney's death. That rat has lived well past her time, and she has had a better life than most of us!

Elaney did cross over and we have received EVP from Cathy telling us that her rat is with her.

Sarah Jane Speaks!

Cathy's cat, Sarah

I now laugh as I think of this story, but for awhile I felt really crazy. All of a sudden, when Cathy's cat Sarah Jane would meow, it sounded like Cathy's voice trying to say something to me. This occurred several times, and each time I tried to brush it off as just a strange occurrence. Then other people began to notice.

I had hired a new cleaning service and after the first cleaning, they left our house never to return. They exited hastily and told me that they had no interest in being in a place with a talking cat. Their first visit was their last.

Months later I was having the house redecorated, and the window treatment crew arrived. I went outside to water my gardens, and when I returned, a man and a woman greeted me at the door with wide eyes. "Miss Martha," they said, "did you know you've got a talking cat?" They told me they had heard someone talking, and when they went into the room where the voice was coming from, they noticed it was the cat. I just laughed and told them her meow sometimes sounded human. It didn't seem worthwhile to go into details with strangers.

Later that summer, my son Marek and his girlfriend Mari came for a visit. I was about to load them up and drive them to the airport when

Mari cornered me in the kitchen to ask if she could talk to me. Of course, I was open to this, thinking perhaps she'd tell me they were planning to marry. Instead she began to tell me that, while I had been at the grocery store the previous day, she and Marek heard someone talking as they were organizing their suitcases. Mari looked downstairs and saw only Sarah. She was puzzled until she realized it was Sarah doing the talking. Then she was shocked!

I asked Mari what Sarah had said, and she said that both she and Marek thought they had heard, *"Marek, Marek, your sister is here."* Then all the lights in the house flickered off and on. She added that Marek had run out of his room saying, "That's Cathy!"

Now I have curious friends who show up just to see if they can hear the talking cat, but Sarah is much too sophisticated to consider herself a circus act. She just stares silently at any curiosity-seekers, knowing full well that if she has an important message for someone special, she is able to deliver it. Meanwhile, I no longer feel crazy about all this.

Dreams of Cathy

October 2, 2002

In my dream I am standing on what appears to be steps covered in a moss-like substance. Others are with me on the steps as well; however, we do not speak to each other. I feel a pulling sensation in my body, much like when I'm standing in the ocean awaiting the next wave. It's explained to me that this is what is known in the spirit realm as a Wave of Consciousness. I'm being told in a telepathic way that one is picked up this way then released to a level that best suits one's vibration rate. As I am lifted away, I see that my physical form, along with the others, is left behind in a sleep state on the steps. There appear to be guards watching over our empty forms.

Martha with Cathy in Ocean with Sumo and Shishi

Continuing to rise and feeling this pull, I can look down and see steps, terraces of the various levels. Each level is unique and earth-like in its own way. Along the way at each level, some people are released from the Wave of Consciousness, gently landing on the terrace below. Each is greeted by a familiar person or persons. I continue to be transported, along with others, via the Wave of Consciousness.

Now I'm looking at a landscape of beautiful, small mountains with cascading waterfalls and exotic flowers, much like Hawaii or some other tropical island. Cathy, waving and smiling, is waiting below me on this terrace. With the feeling of being released, I slowly float down toward her, joining her on the steps. The Wave of Consciousness continues without me, still carrying people to the next levels.

Cathy introduces me to her friends Rob and Jamie. I'm aware of these friends because of previous (pre-dream) conversations with their mothers on the phone. (Their stories appear in Part 2: The Big Circle.) Cathy is excited and talking a mile a minute. She explains to me that our physical bodies on earth were able to stay there grounded because of gravity. Without physical forms and gravity, she tells me, each soul will simply stay where its vibration rate is best suited. She has excitedly repeated what had been explained to me earlier. Cathy further explains that anyone can certainly visit the other levels, depending on vibration rate and the intervals between Waves of Consciousness. She says this is similar to how voice transmitting works. I know that she means EVP. This explains why the messages we receive from beyond are usually faint and brief. It has to do with vibration.

I notice that the love surrounding me with Cathy and her friends at this level provides me with a sense of gravity, which allows me to remain for a longer visit. Rob points toward his grandfather Opa, who is somewhat visible, but appears to be waving to us from the background. Opa wants Rob's mother, Karen Mossey, to know that he is with Rob, but they have separate lifestyles, just as on the physical plane.

Cathy, Rob, Jamie, Lance and other young people, whom they seem to know, express how happy they are in their new environment. They talk about being surrounded by extreme joy, love and beauty. Much concern is still felt for loved ones left behind on the physical plane. Strong awareness of the emotions we feel on Earth seems to be deeply absorbed by souls at this level. Together they seem to be working to narrow that gap between our dimensions, something which was never possible before.

There seems to be an overwhelming desire among these young people to provide a reliable method for filtering through to us their emotions of peace, joy and happiness. They communicate that they are able to pick up on what emotions we are experiencing in our world. By sending to us their joy and peace, they hope to relieve some of the pain and negative feelings to which we subject ourselves. I understand that these messages from beyond, expressing the importance of soul growth, are necessary for all dimensions. If any goal to continue to grow spiritually is not achieved at one level, it seems that all levels suffer. Our young souls in the hereafter are much more advanced in technical ways than ever before, but for them to succeed in their mission, we must offer our complete cooperation.

Cathy tells me I must return soon, but first takes my hand, and we rise together into the Wave of Consciousness. Then we are lowered onto steps of another level. Shishi, our former dog, greets us, followed by another former pet, Muffin. Both are young again, and both seem equally happy to see me. They begin to perform the tricks they once did before they became old and sick.

As the invisible wave sensation begins again, Cathy's face rises into it, leaving me behind. She continues glowing and smiling down at me, then she disappears from sight. Before I can wave goodbye, I am picked up, too, only to be released at the level where I had abandoned my physical form. As I return to my body, the pulling sensation of the Wave of Consciousness is replaced by the gravitational pull on my physical body.

I notice that other people are returning to their physical bodies, too, in much the same way. We still do not speak to each other, and some have a look of confusion on their faces. However, I do notice a man and woman embracing each other. As she waves to him, she turns away, and he joins us by returning to his physical form on the steps.

I awaken in my bed and notice the time is 3:43 A.M.

October 4, 2002

In my dream I am walking with Cathy in a meadow, surrounded by all our family animals that are now deceased—quite a herd! We are discussing the fact that some family members are concerned that I might be spending too much time trying to communicate with her, thinking this might not be healthy.

Cathy smiles, then laughs, replying, "Well, Mom, look at it this way: If you were doing studies on exploration of space or the ocean floor, would that be okay with other people? Think about it in these terms: Billions of dollars are spent on exploring both these areas, and how many people will ever get to go there? Sooner or later, we will all end up here, so why not be better prepared?"

I have to smile back at her. I'm noticing that she is aglow, and we are surrounded with vivid colors and smells. She continues, "Mom, every trip or move you've ever made was well-researched before you went. Isn't this the same? What's the big deal? What is creepy about wanting to know what your last move, your last trip will be like?"

Now I'm laughing, and she just carries on. "There will be those who don't do their homework. They might refer to those who do as being weird or morbid. You've always been both a worrywart and a nosey person, so why stop now?" It's true that my curiosity had often gotten the best of me. Cathy reminded me of more: "Remember when I moved into that townhouse? You came to check it out. I know you did this because you loved me, so why would this be any different?"

Cathy in Ocean with Donna

This is all I remember of the dream, but I'm pretty sure I awoke smiling. Since then, I've often reminded people that it *does* make sense to explore the area to which we're all bound to travel.

Home Movies

It's like a longing for a specific food. On some days when I pull out the old home movies and plug them into the television, I'm heartened and entertained by watching Cathy on the screen. One of my favorites is a video that Cathy made with a friend for a school project. In it, she has dressed up various family pets as sumo wrestlers, and her friend is an announcer who, in true tabloid television style, announces how this pet is going to "pulverize" that pet in an upcoming event. They give details about the "fighting weight" and characteristics of each animal "star." This movie just makes me laugh out loud—and sometimes cry—every time I see it. It reminds me what a truly original and brilliant person Cathy was …and is.

I think I love the experience of watching home movies because I miss her voice and laughter. I sometimes forget the little things about her. She used to bite her fingernail on her baby finger when she would get nervous. Seeing her face on the screen reminds me of these things. As I proceed through the grieving process, I am afraid I will forget her character, her personality and her funny faces for the movie camera.

I will admit I have mixed emotions in all this. I feel happy because in the movies I realize she did have a wonderful life, and I did everything possible to make her life comfortable and beautiful. I realize I wasn't a failure; her death is something I could never have prevented.

Sometimes I feel sad, filled with grief because it will be a long time before we are really together again, and I have to get up every day knowing this is the way it has to be. This is such a feeling of powerlessness. There is nothing I can do about it but just get through the days, get through the years.

Most of the time when I'm watching home movies, I feel a tinge of guilt. I wish I had made more of them. Perhaps I got lazy near the end of her life, didn't take as many as I should have. Then I sigh with relief, because in many ways, I have more of Cathy's presence in my life than many parents do. At least I do get to hear her voice rather often, I do have her in my dreams, and sometimes like this morning, when I'm in the kitchen playing with her dog Doja and my dog Shorty, I catch a glimpse of her watching us.

In this glimpse, as usual, Cathy is smiling. I stop and smile back, and by the time I am able to say, "I love you Cat," she has faded away and is gone again.

I remember that Cathy once explained to me in a dream why most people are not interested in exploring the spiritual world. She used the comparison of my pets representing what we think of as the "physical realm," with me and Don being the "spiritual realm." My pets feel happy and safe in their little world, with very little need for things to be different when their basic needs are met. But we know our world is much more complex than our pets' world. Shorty and Doja's minds are not capable of understanding our world, although I'm not so sure about Sarah Jane the cat. Still, both worlds do exist at the same time and together, but our pets do not have that awareness. I thanked Cathy for this analogy, and look forward to the day when I can leave the Shorty and Doja's world and join Cathy in her new world.

Signs from Cathy in Pictures

Cathy's graduation picture (inset) and her picture in a December 25, 2001 memorial. Note the streak across Cathy's face in the memorial picture.

I wrote this on October 8, 2002:

> We are in Virginia visiting our friends Cindy and Norm Martel. They show me a picture of Cathy they had taken. In their photograph was Cathy's graduation picture. They had placed it on a table along with candles I had given to Cindy. On Christmas Eve Cindy's family members each lit a candle in remembrance of Cathy. Norm had told Cindy that she should take a picture of Cathy's portrait with the candles lit and send it to me. Cindy took one picture, then decided to take another one in case the first one did not take. The first picture was perfect and clear, but the second picture appeared to have a white streak across Cathy's face. The lighting, distance and perspective were the same as the first picture, and it was taken immediately after the first picture. Norm felt it was Cathy's spirit visiting them to thank them for remembering her on Christmas.

Don and Martha.
The bright area over Martha's face is believed to be a moving orb

The second sign was similar. My mother gave me a picture that was taken in June at my sister Donna's house while my aunt and cousin were visiting. We were sitting in the dining room, and I was looking down with a smile and my eyes closed. In the picture, it looks like the most peaceful expression on my face (rare for me). You can see the same streak of light across my face as the one in the picture taken by Cindy.

Then at home I found the third sign, a picture my son had taken of Cathy climbing into the driver's side of her car. The same light can be seen, located at the same spot on her head that hit the windshield during her fatal accident.

Continuation of Signs from Cathy

Yesterday at my Buford Presbyterian Church, in Buford, Georgia, I met a couple whose son had been killed two weeks earlier in an automobile accident. They told me that he was already sending them "signs" from beyond to comfort them.

It is so important to pay attention to "signs" that our loved ones send to us from spirit. Just today, while searching through photo albums for pictures to insert in this book, I found a "sign" from Cathy. It was an album she had made for my fiftieth birthday party entitled "The Way it was." It contained all the important facts and events from the 1950s, along with photos of me when I was a baby up to my present life. One thing that really struck me in this album was her dedication page. It read:

> My dedication goes to my mom, Martha Pierce Copeland.
> *Hope is the destination that we seek,*
> *Love is the road that leads to hope*
> *Courage is the motor that drives us*
> *We travel out of darkness into faith*
> *-The Book of Counted Sorrow*

How very strange to be reading these words now. Although going through the old photo albums made me sad, perhaps this is Cathy's "sign" for me to continue on and have faith in what the future holds.

"Tears in Heaven"

Today I was riding in the car, listening to the CD of music we had played at Cathy's funeral. Each song was chosen for a specific story in her life, and each one usually brought tears to my eyes. When Eric Clapton came on singing, "Tears in Heaven," I remembered the first time I heard it.

Cathy was about ten years old, and we were living in Okinawa, Japan, on the military base. Two of the children she often played with were twins, a girl and a boy, Shane and Shannon. One day while Cathy was playing with them, Shane was hanging upside down by his knees from a tree limb, hitting at the girls as they rode by on their bicycles. Something caused him to lose his grip, and he fell to the ground. His head hit the curb. Cathy came running home and said, "Mom, I think Shane is dead." He was taken to the hospital where he died shortly from his injuries.

The day of Shane's memorial service, Cathy had picked up her room, making it spotlessly clean. This was unusual for our girl, whose bedroom floor was rarely seen. We went to the service and joined the grieving family and friends of this young boy. The song, "Tears in Heaven," was too poignant and left everyone weeping as we said goodbye to Shane.

We had been home from the service a few hours when cars started pulling up in front of our house, and parents let out their children. At least thirty children had shown up, and Cathy was at the door greeting her friends. Even Shane's twin sister Shannon was there. When I asked what was going on, she informed me, "Mom, I told them that you were going to have a séance and bring Shane back to talk to us." I was stunned and told her that I was absolutely not going to do that.

Cathy, "my little psychic."

Cathy glared at me, grabbed her Ouija board and stormed off to her room, closing the door behind her after the many kids piled inside. While my "little psychic" was in there, I glimpsed Shane in our living room. He was wearing a blue and white striped shirt with cut-off jeans.

Cathy later reported that she and her friends had asked some questions of her board, and had gotten some "yes" answers, which helped them believe that they had contacted Shane. This must have helped the grieving process for these youngsters, who needed a chance to say goodbye to their little friend. I asked Cathy what Shane had been wearing at the time of his accident. She described his outfit just as I had seen in my living room.

"Would you know my name … if I saw you in heaven?" As I listen to these plaintive phrases sung by a man who was a grieving parent, I know the answer to the question he poses. I know without a doubt that we will recognize our loved ones when we get to the Other Side. Still, this thought does not stop the tears I have here and now.

Gettysburg fun with EVP

Once my sister, Ginny, and I went to Gettysburg with Karen Mossey, her friend, Mike Sullivan, and his friend, John. John brought a beat-up old van and drove us all around town. Now, both Karen and Mike have done a *lot* of EVP recording, and Mike has a very personal relationship with his recorder. He has this habit of saying, in this very earnest and dramatic bass voice, "Helloooooo my friends. How are you all doing out there? I've missed you. I'm sorry I've neglected you and I'm wondering how you're doing." We'd all laugh about it.

At one point on the trip, we were lost and we were all wondering how we might find our way back to where we were supposed to be. "Let me consult my spirit friends. *They'll* help us," Mike said as he picked up his recorder. His big burly friend, John, said, "Just cut it out with the spirit friends stuff!"

Later, Ginny and I were alone, and we were snickering and laughing about who knows what when Ginny grabbed her recorder and said into it very Mike-like, "Well helloooooo my friends, how are you today? I've missed you ...." And we just laughed and laughed. When we played it back, there was some silence after Ginny's address, then we heard a clear voice say, ***"Cathy's here!"***

Our eyes flew wide. "We've got to let Karen hear you!" I said. "Wait!" Ginny said, "Mike can't hear this! He'll be mad that I'm making fun of him."

When we played it back for Karen, Mike and John, Mike said, "You're copying my technique. That's sweet!" Then he heard the snickering. His friend was laughing so hard that Mike finally said, "Wait a minute! You're actually making fun of me!" He saved that tape, and now when he sees Ginny, he says, "I've still got that tape."

Part 2

The Big Circle Evolves

Discovering the AA-EVP

After hearing Cathy's voice coming through the computer, I did some research on the Internet to find out more. I wanted some definitions about this contact experience I was having with Cathy. What was this all about? I found my favorite search engine, and then typed into the computer "After Death Communications." I came up with many well-known mediums and psychics. There was also a long list of books pertaining to after-death communications. Scrolling down the informative web page, I spotted a group called the American Association of Electronic Voice Phenomena (AA-EVP). Reading their main web page, I realized this group might be able to help me with my communications with my daughter. So I decided to join. I immediately placed a check into the mail addressed to the AA-EVP and covering membership for both my sister Ginny and me.

Ginny had been recording with me every Thursday, an incredible gesture of love and support. As we began to explore the AA-EVP website, Ginny and I first observed what the on-line members were discussing. Most of the time, we were really clueless as what they were talking about. I noticed that various names kept recurring: Mike Sullivan, Karen Mossey, and Erland Babcock would send emails on topics like "wave files" and "converting files to mp3 wave files." I had no idea what "wave files were," nor anything about the software they were using to "filter" their recorded clips. If that were not bad enough, now and then Tom Butler would join in and add technical information. Ginny and I would read his emails with blank expressions on both our faces.

It was while visiting my dearest and most longtime friend (a friendship going back to third grade) Irene Matzgannis in Newport News, Virginia, that I finally got the nerve to send an email to this Karen Mossey person with the AA-EVP group. Karen seemed to be the person in charge of an online email sharing group, and in one of her emails I noticed that she had mentioned losing her son Rob from a brain seizure.

I've discovered there is a special bond that exists between mothers who have lost children, a bond that cannot be explained. When we contact each other, a deep understanding seems to occur immediately. This was certainly the case when Karen and I began to communicate. Below is some email correspondence Karen and I have exchanged. Needless to say, there have been many more since these:

=====Email=====

Karen,

My session with George Anderson was amazing! (Everyone in my family listened to the taped recording and cried.) It was so-o-o-o CATHY.... he hit on things that nobody else could know about. ~ Martha

=====Email=====

Martha,

*That's because Cathy was telling him. I am reading his book right now, **We Don't Die**. I also read his book **Lessons from the Light**. I am so happy that your session was so very enlightening. This is the validation that we need to let us know our loved ones live on in spirit. I lost my twenty-three-year-old son Rob in 2000, Martha, so I can feel the emptiness in your heart. It never leaves—it just becomes that which we now have to bear and live with forever.*

My belief in the afterlife is very strong; that is why I do research in the AA-EVP. I have had too many signs from my son to believe otherwise. He is very definitely with me, as Cathy is with you. I have also been to three amazing mediums, and Rob came through with every one of them. They say he is a very highly-evolved soul. Though many tears flowed, a sense of peace and comfort knowing that he lives on in his world helped me so much. I continue to go, and continue to seek more understanding of the afterlife. It is good to surround yourself with spiritual people and those who comfort you; be of strong heart to go

through your life in your own way and at your own pace, and let no one tell you otherwise. Believe, and may the blessing of spiritual knowledge be with you.
    Very Sincerely, Karen

=====Email=====

Karen,
    Thanks Karen, I am very sorry to hear about your son but was wondering if you have received any messages from him by using the computer? ~ Martha

Karen Mossey with her children at Rob's grave. Left to right: Karen, Sean, Alex. Jessie and Conner

=====Email=====

Martha,
    No, not yet, but I have received several other signs to let me know he is around. Can you briefly let me know how I would go about setting up to receive signs from him on the computer? Have you gotten signs from Cathy? I am very interested. Thank you, Martha.
    ~ Karen

=====Email=====

Karen,

My niece was the first one to receive a message from Cathy. Cathy has given me several since that time. One recent sign was an EVP of her voice, saying she had Muffin (her dog that died right after she was killed) with her, and you could hear the dog making a noise in the background.

My niece got her just using Windows Media Player on her computer, but it was not as clear as when I can use [the editing software] Cool Edit. I do not yet own the Cool Edit program, but have been using another one called Magi Audio Cleaning Lab.

I found lighting a white candle, using my storm lamp, and having her picture by the computer seems to help. (I would stand on my head if that would work!) Her voice is very faint and quick, and we have to play it back several times to make out what she is saying. I have had several people in the room who have heard her recorded voice.

I am not in Georgia right now, but will return home tomorrow night. Perhaps we both can try to contact your son. Cathy's birthday is September 26; she would have been twenty-one years old. So I plan to try to reach her, and will let you know if I have any luck. It is wonderful to hear that voice, so keep trying and it will happen! ~ Martha

=====Email=====

Hey Martha,

I am so encouraged by what you have told me. I keep thinking that some of the EVP I have received on my DR60 are Rob, but because of a distortion in the way the voices come across, I can't seem to confirm it. I am still trying more filtering. I lost my dad four weeks ago, and Rob was his first grandson, and they were so close here on Earth that I know without a doubt they are together. I just keep trying to get a message from them. The other day I asked who I was speaking with, and I am almost sure that the message was "Robert Browning (my son's name) and Opa" (that is what we called my dad—it's the German name for Grandpa). I felt it had to be them, as who else would refer to my dad as Opa? I am going to look into getting that program, the audio cleaning lab you mentioned, and I would consider it a wonderful gift if you or anyone who wishes could attempt to contact Rob. I am also going to get a storm lamp like yours. I don't have one. I light *a candle every night for my son and dad, so that is a given. I have been so lifted up by this note from you. Please stay in touch. I also belong to the Compassionate Friends group in my area. This is a group of parents that have lost children. Rob's birthday is October 23rd. He will be 25. Please even feel free to call me anytime. I will light a special candle for Cathy on Thursday the 26th—and HAPPY 21st Birthday, Cathy. I can't express how comforted and encouraged I am by your letter.*

Sincerely, Karen

=====Email=====

Karen Mossey with her Alex and Sean
on a visit to Georgia to meet Martha

Karen,

My sister Ginny just called me and said that she received a "Class A" message from Cathy. Ginny said into her recorder, "I miss you Cathy" and heard Cathy reply, "I miss you too, Ginny." Tomorrow is Thursday, so Ginny will come over to my house to record with me for what we feel Cathy would refer to as "Psycho Sisters Day!" I will email you if we receive anything.

For some reason it seems we receive more EVP messages from Cathy about the middle part of the month. ~ Martha

=====Email=====

Karen,

The weirdest thing (other than me) happened today while I was eating breakfast in my kitchen. I have the two goldfish from my pond in a tank in my kitchen. (I had to move them inside until my outside house painting is completed) The pump on the tank started sounding like it was saying, "Cathy's with Opa." I had to get away from the house for the entire day, then felt really bummed out about it. I don't understand why I felt that way! It was a very restless feeling that I can't explain. ~ Martha

=====Email=====

Martha,

They can talk through the pump. Remember how Charli talked through her coffee pot? I believe you did hear that. Love, Kare

=====Email=====

Karen,

In a dream with Cathy last night, she told me that Rob would stop butting into my recordings once we figured it all out! ~ Martha

=====Email=====

Martha,

Your EVP of a young male's voice saying, "Marvin" was sent through you by my son Rob as a strong clue to me that this message was from him. Rob always called my dog Merlin "Marvin." I used to tell him to stop calling him Marvin because he was going to make him not know his real name, and he would just laugh and keep calling him "Marvin." Maybe Marvin is a sign to me from Rob—a sign just I would understand and know that it is him.

Cathy and Rob know they can send this through either of us because we are close and both will understand. This is all part of their plan, a bigger plan, part of which was our meeting each other. It is important that a message that comes to any of us, if we feel it has significance to anyone in The Big Circle, be sent to the group. The message may not personally be for the one receiving it, but you can bet it is meant for someone in the group. Their awareness of the total is greater then ours. They see beyond what our physical eyes see. Rob and Cathy know we are "figuring it out." But here on the physical we are a bit more "dense" (no pun intended, but the truth is) and things take us longer.

Love, Kare

=====Email=====

Karen,
   I think I may have received an EVP from George Wynne's wife Maya on my recorder last night. Could you listen to my clip and let me know what you hear?
   Thanks, Martha

=====Email=====

Martha,
   I could hear "Maya Wynne" and "Maya" very clearly. Congratulations to George for aiding as a conduit to bring her through. All your work brings tears of joy to my heart.
   Cathy is so beautiful! Thanks for sharing the photo of her at the computer. I feel like I know her... ~ Kare

Maya and George Wynne

The Recording Circle Takes Form

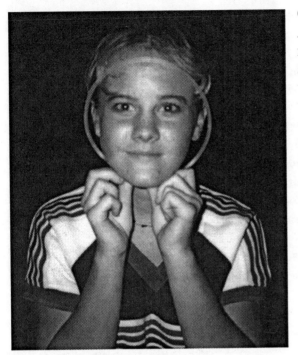

Eleven years old Cathy

Other members in the AA-EVP started emailing me privately; inquiring about the techniques I used to bring Cathy's voice through the recorder. I realized then a need to establish a special group, separate from the ordinary e-group. I emailed Lisa Butler, co-director of the AA-EVP, to ask if she knew of anyone in our group who had formed a pact whereon if a person did cross over, they would contact the person left behind. My thoughts were that someone must have encountered a phenomenon like this, much in the same way that my niece Rachel had done with Cathy before Cathy's death.

Lisa must have misunderstood what I was saying, because she emailed me back a beautiful and compassionate letter about why I must not consider taking my own life. Embarrassed by this misunderstanding, I just let it slide but continued wondering if this had ever happened to others.

Meanwhile, I spent a lot of time answering emails from many people who had lost loved ones. Often they would tell me how much hearing Cathy's voice helped their grief. Many, like me, had tried other avenues of grief support groups only to discover that these provided very little comfort. So I told my stories as a means to comfort them and began to think in many directions about how we culturally understand death. I knew from George Anderson's work that contact with one's deceased loved ones had long been known as an effective form of grief therapy. I wanted to help others with this.

I felt Cathy did not care if I celebrated her birthday with a cake, ate her favorite foods or played her favorite CD's. These were things of the physical plane that no longer met her needs. Cathy's contacts with me were happening to help me and other grieving parents realize this: "Death isn't the end, but a transition into the next stage of life. Our loved ones are still around from time to time, and yes, they get busy over here, too." It is our loved ones in spirit who pray for us. To me it seems they want us to open our minds and try to establish some form of communication with them. They're just awaiting our efforts.

Cathy: "Like living but better."

We have to learn how to undo the ways we perceive the death experience in our society. Death to us is black and creepy. We feel that the corpse represents the end of that person we loved. We are taught that after-death communications are wrong and unnatural. We somehow believe that the person we loved was their body, which has ceased to exist, not their spirit, which continues on. After all, we are spirits just trapped in a physical body.

Interestingly, it was my daughter who first made contact with us to let me know she was all right. I felt no guilt in receiving her message, rather a sense of pure joy in hearing her voice again. It's too bad for those who still hold the death experience in medieval terms of the Dark Ages. As Cathy has reminded us, millions of dollars are wasted on space exploration and ocean research, but how many of us will ever walk on the moon or the bottom of the ocean? One thing is for sure: We will all be walking in the spiritual world someday! Just imagine how our world would be if money were spent on researching the after-life. What might we do with access to famous and great minds such as Einstein, Edison, etc.?

So why are we afraid to explore our new world? If this place is supposed to be *heaven,* why are people so turned off by ideas about it? Many of us already have friends, animals and family members we love over there, so what are we afraid of? Perhaps it's simply this: people are afraid of the unknown.

As I considered all these questions, and perhaps a few I haven't begun to articulate, I felt it was time to find the right kind of group, even if I had to start it myself. There had to be other curious minds out there, and I wanted to join with like minds, open-minded individuals who shared my feelings of the importance of searching for ways to establish communications with the spiritual world. Love is the most important and powerful tool in aiding in this communications. The private emails I received from others who were also searching for proof that their loved ones were okay made me realize that there was a real need for a special group of bereaved persons. We would be *pioneers* of our time, and what we learn might forever change how we all view death!

So I decided to start a group and call it "Recording Circle–Bridge to the Afterlife." This would be the method for communicating with our loved ones; those in spirit whom we have heard call themselves "The Big Circle." My decision was finalized after discussing this with Karen Mossey and my sister Ginny. They both agreed that this could be a break-through for our society. Karen Mossey offered her support to be my partner in this undertaking (no pun intended).

I have learned many things about spiritual work from my contacts with Cathy. When I have asked her what her new world was like, her reply was, *"Like living but better."* Cathy has told me that there are clouds in heaven.

Our Recording Circle–Bridge to the Afterlife group is growing in number and EVP has attracted the attention of Universal Studios, which released a film on this topic in early 2005. I, along with other AA-EVP members were a part of a movie trailer for *White Noise*, starring Michael Keaton. The footage was filmed at the AA-EVP conference in the summer of 2004. The educational featurette helped teach the public about EVP by showing the more factual and positive aspects of EVP. The movie is a psychology thriller that does not portray EVP accurately. As I write the book I am being told that more information from the AA-EVP conference will be included in the DVD version In the future, we think grief professionals may even use our methods of EVP in helping to enhance the process of healing from grief.

Recording Circle Details

We receive many inquiries from people all over who have come to the AA-EVP website and wish to connect with others who are grieving, as well as to network with our group, Recording Circle - Bridge to the Afterlife. Here is Karen Mossey's email exchange with a woman named Patti:

Karen: *Welcome to our world, Patti. I will try to answer some of your questions.*

Patti: *I am absolutely fascinated with the idea of getting a group of people together specifically for the purpose of recording EVP. For those who are currently sitting in such a group, could you give me some information about your group? Where do you meet?*

Karen: *We have a meditation circle which we call "Recording Circle - Bridge to the Afterlife." It extends all over the country and involves a coming together of anyone in the group or family/friends who wish to record or meditate in an effort to reach our loved ones through EVP or meditation.*

Patti: *Do you change locations?*

Karen: *Location is wherever you are and can participate. Martha conducts hers in a darkroom which her husband Don built for her. This is similar to a psychomanteum.*

Patti: *How often do you meet?*

Karen: *Usually every other Thursday. Tomorrow is one of those Thursdays.*

Patti: *Do you meet at a set day and time?*

Karen: *Usually every other Thursday at 8:00 P.M. EST*

Patti: *How many people are there in your group? How many usually attend a session? AND WHERE DID YOU FIND THEM???*

Karen: *No set number. Just whoever wishes to participate. Participants tend to be AA-EVP members, relatives or friends of current group members.*

Patti: *Do your sessions have a set order?*

Karen: *We begin at 8:00 P.M. EST. First we read through our spiritual roster of names of loved ones on the Other Side. Then we record and meditate for 10 minutes. We then usually do a brief review of that session, and then conduct one more ten- minute session.*

Patti: *Is there a designated leader for the session?*

Karen: Martha Copeland founded the group, but we are all part of *The Big Circle.* I will generally send an email reminder a half-hour before the session begins to anyone who has requested to be included.

Patti: Does this change for each session? How many people are taping during the session? When do you review the tapes?

Karen: No, it doesn't change unless indicated. Sometimes we have to change the day or time, but we try to be consistent. I believe the spirit world appreciates this consistency as they are working to a schedule as well and since they, as we, have work to do, it is a time they can plan on.

Patti: Anything else I should know??? (I guess it shows that I am eager for information.)

Karen: Join us if and when you are able. We would benefit from your energy, especially considering your expertise and fields of study and practice. Follow the emails. A most warm welcome to you. Love, Karen

The Spirit Room

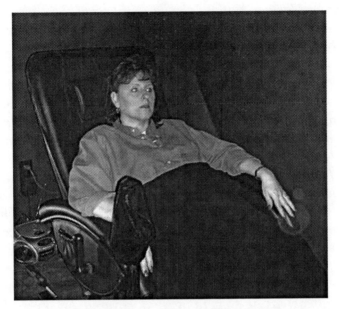

Judy Quillen in the "Spirit Room."

My husband Don has been kind enough to help me renovate our basement to use for the Recording Circle activities. I have electric candles and rainbow lights on alternating stairs going down to the basement. You first enter a sitting area where we gather for our Thursday sessions. Then there is a small room off this area which we call the Spirit Room. It is painted entirely black and is furnished with only a small electric candle, a wax candle and a black leather massaging recliner. An oval mirror with a small white dot on it faces the recliner. This type of room is known as a psychomanteum, so named by the ancient Greeks to describe a room where spirits were summoned.

I have captured considerable EVP and ITC (Instrumental TransCommunication) examples in the Spirit Room. On one occasion when I decided to take pictures with Judy Quillen there, I recorded images of several spirit orbs. (Orbs are believed to be how spirits show up in photographs. More can be learned by researching ITC at www.aaevp.com and other sites.) First, I'll include Judy's narrative of her experience that day, which she emailed to me:

Hi, everyone ~ The memory of this experience was great! Martha, did we get any orbs in the pictures? Just curious!

After Martha, Kathy Malone and I went through our relaxation and meditation session, I went into Martha's Spirit Room. I really LOVE her room and want to make one in my basement! We put our recorders on a table in the room outside her Spirit Room. Cat's Ouija board was on the table beside Martha's laptop, so I put my recorders on top of the board. I went into the room, and Martha lit the candle, then turned on the electric candle and a small flashlight. Then she started the meditation tape and left.

I began calling my daughter Jamie by her full name, stating I wanted to make contact with her. Almost immediately one of the lights went out. That is her way of letting me know when she is around. I began my deep breathing and concentrating on the mirror. All at once, the room went totally black. I could see nothing, but my eyes were wide open. I blinked a couple of times to make sure of the reality, and then noticed the lights were there. It was almost as if something had covered my eyes. I was not scared and felt no fear.

I really began to concentrate on the mirror, which made my eyes begin to sting. I could see an image of Jamie's face forming, but it never became clear because I had to blink often to focus. A tear ran down my left cheek, and I was very aware of it as it moved down my face. I made no attempt to wipe it away. I was not crying, nor did I feel sad, just uncomfortable. As I continued focusing on the mirror, I saw a small light (orb?) on the wall to the right of the mirror. It quickly flew under the mirror to the left side on the wall beside me. Then it flew across the mirror, and I felt as though a presence was in the room.

Martha knocked on the door then, but I did NOT want to stop. I really wonder what would have happened if I had stayed longer. Is there a limit to the amount of time one should spend in the Spirit Room?

Needless to say, I got some interesting messages on my recorder! A lot of loud noises that I couldn't make out. I got one "I love you...." Thanks everyone! ~ Judy

As Judy mentioned, I entered the room with a camera and took 11 shots. Five of them revealed spirit orbs. The first appeared behind the chair in a frame with Judy in it, and then I photographed Judy as she was describing her experience to me, and two orbs appear behind her head. I continued to snap pictures, and as she was telling me that the mirror seemed to form a mist, the photograph shows a small orb forming by Judy's left arm, about where her sleeve and skin met. The last one is a most awesome picture! It appears that Judy is holding Jamie's hand, and there is another small orb beside Jamie. Two orbs are forming over Judy's head, and another two in front of her face. Then when one looks at the right of the picture, there is a small orb near the top and one below.

Karen then sent around the following email about the ancient art of mirror scrying:

Martha, Andrea, and anyone else...

Here is a quote from "Methods of Psychic Development" by Dr. Quantz Crawford. I suggested to Martha that she try this in her psychomanteum room. He is talking about a relatively inexpensive mirror, concave with a black background. Size is not too important. Here is his suggestion:

"In the use of a mirror, certain preparations are necessary. You want to acquire a good grade of mirror, not necessarily expensive, but one that is of good grade. Then you want a little room—the room you use for your development and practice is sufficient. Put the mirror on the wall, then place a little desk or stand right under the mirror. Get a little piece of white paper. Cut out a bit the size of a pea and paste it in the center of the mirror ... the little piece of paper will match the center of your forehead, between the eyes, at the root of the nose.

"After having done all this, you use a candle. All the lights in the room are to be out. Use a candle large enough so that you don't have to light it every so often or worry about it going out. Place this candle to the left side of your stand so that just a slight reflection of it lights your face in the mirror. Do not let your eyes deviate in any way. Think of nothing. Just hold your whole attention on this little white spot. When you begin to see things in the mirror, keep your eyes and attention on the white spot; don't try to see anything with your physical eyes. You will be doing the

seeing with your inner eyes, your subtle eyes. So regardless of what appears in the mirror, do not become startled or surprised. Just continue to look at the white spot. The white spot will disappear when the development in the mirror is sufficiently clear, so that the image will be seen in the mirror instead of anything else.

"Your face will disappear; you will only see the image in the mirror. You might see letters, perhaps so clearly that you will actually be able to read the words; you might see faces or pictures of various things; you might see someone who has passed; you might see someone you know or don't know who is at a distance..."

Dr. Crawford believes it is important to practice this for at least ½ hour during each meditation, and goes further to say we can find answers to our questions through this method. Anyway, I wanted to share this. ~ Karen

Raymond Moody's Psychomanteum Experiments

I wanted to know more about this method, so I inquired on the Internet. At www.som.org, I found an interview with the famous afterlife researcher, Dr. Raymond Moody, on precisely this topic. In the text he relates this:

"I set up a situation in my own research facility; I built a chamber [with] a mirror surrounded by a black velvet curtain, and arranged in such a way so that a person sitting in the booth does not see their own reflection, but a clear optical depth....

"I set it up, tested it out. I assumed that maybe about one of ten subjects would have some experience, but immediately it became obvious that it was going to be at least 50%. Much to my astonishment, the apparitions were experienced as real events, especially [significant] since I was using as the subjects my own colleagues, psychologists, and my own graduate students of psychology. I assumed that anybody who saw anything would say, 'Yeah, you know, I saw an image, it looked like my grandma, but I don't know if it was real or a figment...'

"In fact, my subjects started coming out of there saying, 'Yeah, I talked to Grandpa,' and it was just astonishing! What we have found is that quite a hefty proportion of the people who see apparitions will actually say that the apparition forms first in the mirror, then emerges from the mirror, comes right out in front of them, full color, three dimensions. Thirty percent of the subjects report hearing the audible voice of the person who has died, carrying on elaborate communications. And, very nicely, the subjects who have been going through this have reported that it helped them with their grief. It helped them tidy up unfinished business. So what I can say for sure is that we have now replicated the common human experience of seeing apparitions of the deceased.

"Well, some people might want to ask, 'Well, is this really the same thing that people are having when they experience apparitions?' Absolutely! If you go back to the early compendia, apparitional tales that were first put together by the Society for Psychical Research a hundred years or so ago, you see that yes, it's very common for people who see spontaneous apparitions first to see them in mirrors or reflective surfaces, and then they come forward. The accounts that subjects give in the psychomanteum... are identical to the accounts we hear from people who have spontaneous apparitions. So, I think we've done it!"

Dr. Moody makes the following recommendations for your scrying inquiry, many of which we discovered on our own prior to this research. For those who wish to establish contact with their loved ones:

◆ Avoid caffeine and dairy products to help your mind get into a serene state.

◆ Go to the quietest part of the house and unplug phones or remove clocks to have a quiet environment.

◆ Gather photos or personal items of the deceased.

◆ Sit in a comfortable position and place a large mirror in front of you.

◆ Create a soft mood by listening to music or looking at pieces of inspirational art.

◆ Gaze into the mirror and wait for it to become cloudy. Your limbs will feel heavy and tingling.

◆ Let information unfold passively; do not ask direct questions.

JoAnne in the Spirit Room

Judy Quillen has a twin sister, JoAnne Windsor, who lost twins shortly after giving birth to them. JoAnne was never allowed to hold the babies, because in those days that was the way hospitals handled situations like this. It's hard to imagine the grief this could cause throughout one's lifetime.

With our group, the Recording Circle–Bridge to the Afterlife that meets at my house on Thursdays, we take turns as to who will sit in the Spirit Room during the session. One week it was JoAnne's turn, and when the recording session ended, Judy took digital photos of JoAnne, which showed spirit orbs forming around her heart.

After the women left my house, I worked on some of their clips by running them through my filtering program, Cool Edit Pro. JoAnne's clip contained many voices, as if there were some kind of roll call going on. In this clip, I could hear Cathy's voice, as well as two little voices, saying "Justin" and "Jessica." These were the names JoAnne had chosen for her twins. Deeply touched by this discovery, I emailed the clip to the group, and other members were able to identify voices belonging to their children, too.

The most comforting result from this experience was that this clip seemed to release some of the heavy burden that JoAnne had been holding in her heart all these years. She never had the opportunity to say "good-bye" to her babies at their deaths.

We have many more examples of amazing things, which have happened to our Recording Circle members using various forms of these methods in my Spirit Room, and we would enjoy hearing your stories at the AA-EVP forum.

Frequency

Cathy December 19, 2001, Martha's parents and Cathy's cousins

I have noticed that there are times when my capacity to reach Cathy is better than others. When I travel, for example, it usually takes a week or two after I return before I can get reliable EVP again. This is also true when I have houseguests or if I'm particularly busy with the tasks of life. At one point I noticed that I had not felt Cathy's presence as close as usual. The EVP I was getting sounded faint and distant. I began wondering if Cathy had moved on to another level in the spirit world, one which was less accessible to me. Did she have to adjust to her new location and a different vibration rate before contacting me again?

About this time my sister Donna asked me if I remembered the Dennis Quaid movie *Frequency*. We had seen it together a few years ago. Its hero was a young man who managed to contact his deceased father (Quaid) by means of a ham radio. I had forgotten most of the story line, but my new interest in EVP prompted me to rent the movie again.

Viewing *Frequency* the second time, I found many symbols relating to my spiritual relationship with Cathy. The most important message occurred when the son was having a particularly difficult time.

He walked into his office and noticed a strange mark on the wooden desk where the ham radio sat. As he looked closer, he realized that the mark was a message burnt into the wood, "I'm still here."

This was the exact phrase I first heard Cathy say on Rachel's computer. Seeing the message there in the movie made my eyes tear up immediately. At that moment, I felt that Cathy, sensing my sadness and the distance from her that I'd been feeling, had somehow planted the idea for this movie in Donna's head. Perhaps this was the only way Cathy could get through to me that she really was "still here," still with me. I realized that perhaps she had been trying to reach me through our established communication paths, but that I had been too busy keeping up with my activities for her to be able to reach me. Maybe I needed to adjust my frequency to again allow communication to flow.

I sometimes notice that when I surround myself with too much "busy-ness" in my life, I build a wall that blocks contact, both with Cathy on the Other Side and with those I love here. Once I realize this, I try to remind myself that all those I love are "still here," regardless of the frenetic pace that might block them out. That realization usually stops me dead in my tracks. I take a deep breath, open my heart, adjust my own frequency, and say to myself, or anyone who's around to hear, "I'm still here."

The Big Circle

Early on in my experiences with recording Cathy's messages to us, she informed us that she identified with what she called The Big Circle. This included both the circle of souls she was coming to know and the circle of friends I was coming to know, each in our respective worlds. It was all one Big Circle. Here are stories from mothers in my part of the Circle, each of whom shares amazing details of interconnectedness and whose children seem to reside in their own part of the Circle.

Vicki Talbott wrote:

> *Hi, everyone. Martha and I have connected about The Big Circle, and in doing so, I shared with her this story. In the past few months I've had the opportunity to speak with two outstanding mediums. Both of them said that my son was saying "Cathy." I don't think he knew a Cathy when he was alive, and when I told this to the mediums, both just said that he was very clearly saying "Cathy," and that he was confident I would figure it out. I have to admit, I hate when they say that!*
>
> *Well, when I found out the role that Martha's daughter Cathy has been playing in the connections between those of us here and those who are there, it all made sense. Braden seems interested in keeping in contact, has probably already met Cathy and friends, and was probably just hoping I'd end up here with your group! ~ Vicki*

Karen Mossey responded:

> *Vicki, it is amazing how our children are still influencing our lives from their world. Martha and I were brought together, too, through the workings of Cathy and my son Rob. If you go to the AA-EVP website and read the story "Children Together on the Other Side," I'm sure you will be assured that your son has indeed influenced you on a path toward this group.*
>
> *We had heard what we thought was the name "Brad" in a previous Recording Circle session, and none of us knew who this might be. The name was not yet on our list. Now we see how this all comes together! Brad was apparently Braden, and he let us know he was part of the circle even before you joined. Now you*

are here. I would not call this meaningless coincidence. I would call this intervention on the part of your son to enable this coming together. Cathy seems to be a very powerful force on the Other Side. She had an existing knowledge of EVP even before she crossed over. ~ Karen

Once I was recording EVP, and I heard the name "Jamie" coming through clearly in a female voice. The only Jamie I know is my nephew, Ginny's son, so I wondered if someone in spirit was joking around. I was confused. A couple weeks later, Judy Quillen called me to ask if I would donate cards for Cathy's first anniversary birthday to Compassionate Friends, a support group for parents who have lost children. Of course, I agreed, and Judy and I continued talking.

Judy told me that she had two daughters with the nicknames "Kat" and "Amos." My daughter had the nickname "Cat," and her last name was Amiss (pronounced just like Amos). We thought this was a wonderful synchronicity, and I invited Judy and her twin sister JoAnne over to my house to record and to hear the voice saying "Jamie." We managed to get the recording a second time. Judy and Joanne agreed that it was their girl's voice saying "Jamie."

Judy wrote this:

Hi, all ~ I went to see John Edward (the famous medium) about four years ago, and my daughter Jamie Ann came through as a "me, too" with another girl. She gave the nickname "Amos" (which is also Martha's daughter's last name, Amiss, hence our connection and deep friendship), as well as my youngest daughter's name, Kathryn (again, Martha's daughter's name is Catherine). Through John we also got very detailed information about Jamie, and a description of Kathryn's room, down to her Pooh collection. Jamie died two days before we moved into our house (see the details at www.jamiequillen.com), and never got to enter this house. Also, Kathryn had just moved into this particular room after my daughter Miranda moved to Dallas. There is no way he could just know these details!

I came away from this visit with a very spiritual "high," so excited about her reaching out to me. That is why I am a member of this group (thanks to Martha's introduction!), and I want to help all grieving mothers to get to this place through their own personal grief journey. I hope I haven't offended anyone, but I guess you have to experience something like this to have the testimony to back it up. ~ Judy

An article in a recent AA-EVP NewsJournal said this about us: "Even if you do not join in the scheduled sessions, we believe that the idea of the 'Big Circle' can become a reservoir in which the energy of love and desire to reach out across the veil can accumulate and thus be available for anyone who seeks to contact a loved one. Using the energy of this growing contact field is easy. Simply conduct your meditations [at the same time as the group] before recording, and visualize yourself and your loved one as part of this family of like-minded friends. Replenishing the energy is also easy. Simply hold a loving thought in your mind for others who share your desire to communicate."

Judy Quillen Remembers
Jamie's Last Day

Jamie Ouillen

Judy Quillen sends this story, which tells many meaningful coincidences about her daughter, Jamie's last day in this reality:

Sunday, February 9, 1997

That day was like any other Sunday, except that it happened to be the last Sunday in the house we had built and lived in for ten years. We were scheduled to move on Valentine's Day, in only five days. All the girls (Amy, 21, Jamie, 20, Miranda, 18, and Kathryn, 13) were to come home that weekend and help pack their respective stuff. Amy was a full time student at Southern Tech in Marietta; Jamie lived with her cousin Kristie in a new apartment in Lawrenceville; Miranda was a senior at Central High; Kathryn was a seventh grader at Crews Middle School.

On this Sunday, I got up and went to church as usual, taught my Sunday school class, and fixed dinner when we got home. Afterward, Jim and I went down to the basement to start going through things, packing what we wanted to keep and tossing out the junk. Amy arrived about 2:00 P.M. and started going through her boxes of school memories. Miranda helped until about 3:00 P.M., and then announced she was leaving to go over to her friend Heather's house. I asked her to call Jamie to find out where she was, and Miranda replied, "Oh, she and Kristie took off this weekend with Sarah to New Orleans for Mardi Gras."

I was furious about this! I fumed to myself, "How could she be so selfish and not be here when I needed her? This was a special weekend, the last that we could all be together as a family in our home. We may never have a chance to come back into this house!" But I knew Jamie, and I'm sure she thought she could get back in time to come over and pack her things. She'd think, "Mom will get over it, just as she always does!"

As I took a box off the shelf, I found Jamie's cast from when she broke her thumb. She is the only child in our family to ever have broken a bone. She was tall, slender, and sometimes clumsy. She had a heart of gold and the biggest eyes, ones that would fill with tears if someone were hurt or sad. She was so sensitive and loving. All her friends and cousins had signed that cast. I smiled as I put it in a box for her.

Next, I found a Ziploc bag with strands of blonde hair, about eight or nine inches long, with a note inside. In Jamie's handwriting, the note held the date of her first 'real' haircut. She was meticulous about dating and recording information. I am so fortunate that she had the foresight to record her special moments in her life!

Going through a lot of storage boxes, I came across Jamie's baby blanket that I had made for her. It wasn't her 'blankie,' that was gone years ago. You see, Jamie sucked her thumb from the time she came home from the hospital. As she did, she rubbed the satin edge of her blankie between her forefinger and other thumb. It was a blue thermal blanket. Everyone fussed at me for not "breaking her of the bad habit" and warned me it would ruin her teeth. Jamie is the only child I had that did not need braces! She had perfect white teeth, the envy of all her sisters.

Into the box went the blanket. As I put the top on the box, I wrote Jamie's name on it. Instinctually, I patted the top of the box. I felt a moment of silliness and wondered why I would lovingly pat this box. Then as I stood up, I got a sharp pull on the left side of my neck. Suddenly I was overwhelmed with a feeling of exhaustion and a need to go the bathroom. I slowly climbed the stairs and as I sat on the toilet, I rubbed my neck while shifting and turning my head. As I went back to the basement door, I called down to Jim, "Honey, let's take a break. I'm tired."

I sat down in my chair with my feet on the ottoman and covered myself with a throw blanket my mother-in-law had given me for Christmas. As I snuggled into the cushions, I turned my head to the right and felt a sharp pain. Turning over to the left I fell into a deep, sleep, the kind of sleep, which has no dreams and makes it hard to wake up. I think Amy left to go back home to her dorm then, too. It was about 4:00 P.M.

After I was fully awake around 7:00 P.M., I gathered my antique clock, and Jim took a few oil paintings, and we walked next door to my twin sister's house. We planned on bringing our prized possessions to the new house in our car. They agreed we could store them there until Friday. My brother-in-law Mark was the only one home. I asked where JoAnne was and he said, "Kristie called, and the car she was riding in broke down somewhere in Mississippi. Jo had to go rescue her and a few of the other kids." I asked why she didn't call me to go with her, and he answered, "Because you were busy packing and Jamie wasn't in the car with Kristie. She left in another car with Sarah and Terry."

He continued, "Kristie is upset because she has been calling their apartment all day, and Jamie hasn't come home yet." I didn't think anything of it, except that maybe they turned around to go find Kristie or had pulled off the road to wait for them to catch up.

It was dark as Jim and I walked back home, and we were holding hands. The air was nippy, and I was aware of the warmth of our hands. I had a fleeting thought, "If Jamie's car broke down, and then she would just have to find another way home. She was supposed to be here this weekend and I'm not driving all over the world to get her!" I knew it was not a valid thought, because I <u>would</u> go to the end of the world to get her! However, later I would remember how heartless that thought was, and the regret of just thinking it would tear through my heart!

I continued to pack up the kitchen and laundry room until about 10:00 P.M. Then I got ready for bed and watched a little TV with Jim. I must have dozed off when I heard the house alarm beep, indicating that someone had opened a door. Miranda wasn't home yet from Heather's house, and I thought it was her. Then I heard a quiet knock on my bedroom door. "Come in," I said. It was my brother-in-law Mark, dressed in his brown robe and slippers. I was surprised to see him. He came over to my side of the bed and sat down at my feet. His hands were in the pockets of his robe.

"I have something to tell you," his voice began to crack. Jim rolled over and sat up in bed. "There was a terrible accident today, and Jamie was killed." I started kicking him with my feet and screaming. "No! No! No! Not my Jamie!" Then I saw headlights from a car coming down the driveway. For a moment I thought it was her. Then Mark told me it was the Gwinnett County Police, and that they have to inform the family when someone dies in an accident. They went to his house by mistake, that is why he knew first. I began pacing between my room and the living room. Kathryn came out of her room and was standing in the upstairs hall that overlooked the living room.

I heard the officer's steps as he came up the front porch. I flung open the door and screamed, "Get off my porch! You have the wrong house!" As I began hitting him on his chest, he grabbed my wrists, and I collapsed to the floor. "My daughter is not dead! She's not dead! You have the wrong house! She's not dead!!" The officer started to cry, too. Mark and Jim brought me back in the house, and Kathryn and I grabbed each other. I began to tremble and shake uncontrollably. I couldn't breathe! My heart was pounding as if I had just run a marathon. Kathryn sat beside me with her hands on her mouth, crying uncontrollably and shaking her head no. Thirteen is such a young and tender age. How she will miss Jamie, growing up without her favorite sister!

Mark brought me back to reality, saying, "We need to call the bishop and the rest of the family. Do you want me to do it?" I just looked at him. He picked up the phone and called our bishop. "Do you want to use Tim Stewart's funeral home?" I responded by just shaking my head yes. They are just down the street, that would be convenient, I thought without really thinking. I felt so confused!

Next Mark called Mom and Pop Quillen. I'm not sure who answered the phone, but when Mark handed it to me it was Pop. I could hear Mom saying, "Oh, my God! Oh, my God," in the background. I don't remember anything else that was said. Amy picked up Miranda from Heather's house and brought her home. We all embraced and nuzzled together, blending our tears in disbelief. One by one my sisters, my mother, my only brother and my cousins arrived. I don't remember anyone talking, just a lot of crying and silence. I think I went back to bed around 5:00 A.M.

Jim was so kind to me. He willingly slept on the couch when I told him I wanted Amy, Miranda and Kathryn to sleep with me. I didn't want to let any of them out of my sight! I am their mother. It's my job to protect them from harm. How could Jamie be dead? How I have failed her!

Monday, February 10, 1997
Slowly during the day, my friends began to come over, Brenda Brown, Melissa Mills, and our Relief Society President, Carol Cheesman. I remember Brenda and Carol packing more house stuff, and Melissa, who is my life long friend since we were three years old, sitting at my feet, holding my hands and telling me how sorry she was. Our real estate agent Jan Edwards came by with her condolences and offers of help. My sisters and brother asked me to look through Jamie's papers and pictures to find things to give the funeral home.

"I just threw out so much of Jamie's school papers! And the negatives to the pictures, I only kept the pictures!" I was so distraught and condemned myself for such a stupid act. The regret began to eat at my stomach and would keep me awake at night for the next six months.

JoAnne had not returned home from picking up Kristie and the other kids. Mark said she had called. They went to Mobile, Alabama, where Willie, the driver of the car that Jamie had been in, was in critical condition. Mike, who was in the car with Kristie, was Willie's best friend and wanted to see him. Then they went to Greenville to look for the car. They were able to get pictures and found Jamie's purse and wallet still in the car! So were her pillow and tennis shoes. The hatchback area, into which Jamie was thrown during the accident, had so much blood! JoAnne knew it was Jamie's blood. I will be forever grateful to my sister for doing this for Jamie and me. It's almost as if Jamie led her to the people who helped her find the car. They said the accident had been the 'talk of the town' all day!

Finally, at about 10:00 P.M., JoAnne and Kristie made it home. JoAnne hugged me and I began trembling and shaking again. She told me all about their trip, meeting Willie's parents (he is an only child), how they saw the accident site, and that Willie's parents had put flowers on the tree. She told me how the car tracks went down the embankment and a large section of tree bark was cut off the tree. She told me how the Mustang had hit the driver's door and wrapped around the tree. She said they took pictures of the tree, too. They looked all around the area for anything that might belong to Jamie, and found a lot of Mardi gras beads, parts of the car, and glass. The ground was soaked in gasoline and oil. I was so glad to have Jamie's shoes and her pillow. One corner had several large bloodstains on it, and I just held it to my face. The smell of her blood made me a little nauseous, but it was all I had of Jamie, so it gave me a small sense of comfort. Kristie gave me Jamie's gorilla. She slept with this soft, plump stuffed animal every night. It became my sleeping companion for the next year.

Tuesday, February 11, 1997

My sister Stephanie arrived from Florida. I rode in her car to the funeral home. I could hardly put one foot in front of the other. "I do not want to do this!" I kept saying to myself emphatically, "It's not right! Jamie is not supposed to die before me!"

At the funeral home I was taken into a conference room and seated in the first chair on the right side of the table. Jim sat beside me, and my family sat around the rest of the table. Mr. Stewart sat at the end of the table next to me. He asked me about family names to be put in the newspaper, where we were going to bury her, and what kind of memorial book I wanted. Fortunately, my family was able to give the correct names and relationships. I had no idea where Jamie would be buried, and I just stared numbly at the different books they put before me. Finally, I picked the pink one with roses on the front. Roses were Jamie's favorite flower.

Then I was escorted into a room with caskets stacked one over the other. They lined the room with two aisles down the middle. I nearly fainted. "I don't want to look at caskets!" my mind screamed, "I just want my little girl back! Don't make me look at these! I just wanted to go backward in time, to force her to come home!" But somehow, I did my duty. I picked out a silver casket with platinum handles and a satin sunburst fabric interior. Next, we must select a cemetery.

We all rode to the Eternal Hills Cemetery in Snellville. My two older sisters have plots there, and I didn't want Jamie to be alone. When we got there, Amy came over to my car and said, "Jamie doesn't want to be here!"

"What are you saying?" I replied.

"She is screaming in my head that she doesn't want to be buried here."

"Then where are we supposed to bury her? The funeral is tomorrow, Amy."

"I don't know. But she is really loud!"

We went into the cemetery office and learned that the salesman was meeting with another family. We filled the room, spilling over the furniture. We waited about twenty-five minutes. During this time Amy kept going in and out of the building. Finally the salesman came out, and we all returned to our cars to look at plots in the back of the cemetery where my sister Carolyn and her husband will be buried.

Amy grabbed me by my arms and shook me hard, "Mom! Jamie doesn't want to be put here! She is yelling at me to go back to Lawrenceville. She wants to be buried in the cemetery down the street from Central High School. The one with three crosses at the entrance."

We finally listened to Amy. As we pulled into the driveway at Gwinnett Memorial Gardens, a peace came upon me. I received confirmation that this is indeed where Jamie wanted to be buried. We picked out eight plots in the Good Shepherd Garden. There are a lot of children buried in this section. Jamie will be at home here.

February 9, 2004

I visit Jamie in the Good Shepherd Garden several times a week, even today after seven years have passed. I love you, my sweet Jamie Ann.

Forever adoring, Mom (Judy Quillen)

Judy wanted to share this poem written by Jamie on: September 14, 1993:

I AM

I am a girl who has ambition.
I wonder if I'll be successful one day.
I hear my Mom telling me to get my education
I see myself starting my life as a flight attendant.
I am a girl who has ambition.

I pretend that I'm a successful actress.
I feel the pain of not succeeding.
I touch my tears as they run down my face.
I worry about not being prepared for an opportunity.
I cry for something exciting to happen in my future.
I am a girl who has ambition.

I understand the fear of losing.
I say you never fail until you stop trying
I dream of traveling to Europe.
I try to reach my goals.
I hope I am successful.
I am a girl who has ambition.
                          Jamie Ann Quillen

I think Jamie has reached her goals, and she is free to travel, or be, whatever she wishes.

Mothers and Others at the Conference

While at the AA-EVP Conference in Reno, Nevada, I had the opportunity to meet in person some of the other mothers belonging to our Recording Circle group. One of the members I had the joy of meeting was Vicki Talbott, who has had several recordings from her home in Washington state with Cathy's voice on them. Vicki was telling me that the night before the conference, she received an EVP from my daughter Cathy saying, "Brain turds." Vicki's eyes danced with delight as she was relaying what she had heard. I just felt my face turning red. If only she knew...

The night before the conference I had stopped by my sister Donna's house because I was nervous about doing the workshop and had hoped she could offer some advice, such as a good escape plan! Lisa Butler, the co-director of AA-EVP, had called me earlier, excitedly informing me that representatives from Universal Studios wanted to film my workshop, "Grief Management Using EVP." The representatives also hoped to conduct a private interview. I had just planned on winging my way through the workshop. Upon leaving Donna's house, I turned to her and said, "I am having major 'brain turds' about this workshop." Donna just smiled at me. Driving back home, I remember thinking, "Gosh, I'm getting old! I meant to say 'brain farts,' not 'brain turds!'"

Now I was smiling because somehow Cathy must have picked up on this. Since I was too busy trying to revise my workshop, she must have come through Vicki's recording, knowing the message would get to me. This was her way of letting me know that she was around me and aware of what was taking place in my life at that time.

I'm so grateful to Vicki for sharing this recording. With this information, I knew that Cathy would be standing right beside me during the workshop, and this eased my tension. After all, I would not want to do anything to embarrass her in front of her spiritual buddies, or as she refers to them, The Big Circle.

Later at the conference, Siobhan McBride told me of several of the EVP recordings that she had received from her son Tony. Siobhan was radiant with calmness and joy as talked about her son.

Judy Quillen, who joins me at my home for the Recording Circle, was also at the workshop. Judy is always so excited when sharing her experiences of communications; whether through EVP or other spiritual signs from her daughter Jamie.

Mary Jo Gran was at the conference, too, and although she has not had as much success as some of the other mother's in receiving EVP messages from her son Jim, she has not given up faith. We all continue to encourage her efforts, because we know that it does pay off. More recently, however, Mary Jo has just started receiving some very clear EVP's from her son Jim.

Lynette Bowers Lovett

Kathy Malone, Lance's mother, presented me with a t-shirt that she had made for me with Cathy's picture on the front and backside. I proudly wore this t-shirt for my workshop and knew Cathy would approve.

Robert Mark Bowers

Kathy Malone and Roddie Eubanks are two more amazing women in our group. These two have suffered the loss of more than one child, but both seem to be at peace with their situations. Kathy Malone attends the recording sessions in my home, and we have had her son Lance's voice come through on several occasions. Roddie Eubanks has had her daughter Lynnette leave a message on her answering machine saying, "I love you."

One mother who was unable to

Tara Elizabeth Jones

attend the conference was Denise Forester, who lost her daughter Tara Jones in an automobile accident. Denise and I keep in contact by private email, and she has told me that she has received 'faint' messages from her Tara.

George Wynne, a close friend of mine, has picked up his wife Maya's voice while we were attending a John Edward show.

Roddie Bowers Eubanks has written to ask that I mention her beloved children, R. Mark Bowers and Lynette Bowers Lovett, in this book. She says, "AA-EVP has brought me up out of the depths of depression. Especially you and Karen."

It continues to fill me with awe and respect that even with faint, weak, or no messages, these people continue to be encouraged by what EVP can offer them. It provides hope and a focus on tomorrow, not yesterday; on possibility, not pain.

Cathy's death has opened a door for helping other people to cope with their grief in a positive manner. We all hope to leave a mark of our existence in the physical world, to feel that we have accomplished a worthwhile deed here before going to our next destination. Cathy and our children in The Big Circle have fulfilled this task.

Karen Mossey and Rob

Robert Benjamin Browning

By now you've heard Karen mentioned quite a few times. Karen is the woman who helped me start the Recording Circle and assisted me with the conference workshop. In fact, the first page of the seminar's workbook tells the story of how Cathy and Rob seemed to bring us together. We've grown to be dear friends through our grief and this work. In the Spring 2003 AA-EVP NewsJournal, Karen is quoted, "I cried reading [Martha's] emails…. I wanted to reach out to her, and there was a driving force that I had to know Cathy. It was stronger than just emailing each other…."

Here are the stories Karen herself tells about contacts with her son since he passed:

> **My son Rob had a brain injury.** He was in an automobile accident at age sixteen, and he went through extensive surgery because of the skull fractures he sustained. On the way to the hospital from the accident, he had three Near-Death Experiences (NDE). He flat-lined three times, but he pulled through. After the reconstructive surgery, he still exhibited frontal lobe syndrome, but the doctor told me he could have a normal life. Along the way, however, he developed seizures.

He was seventeen when this first happened, and we put him on Dilantin. It would keep the seizures in check, but he'd still get some now and then. He'd go down, and it'd be pretty scary. He wouldn't remember anything, just lose all control. But he'd always come back. One day he called me, and he said, "Hi, Mummy." I said, "What's up?" He said, "I'm going to have a seizure."

I wasn't willing to believe him, and I said, "No, you're not." I went over to his house and watched him take his medication. He seemed happy as could be. The next day he had planned an outing with one of his friends. They went bicycling, fishing and swimming. When it was time to go, Andy pulled the car around while Rob went to get his tackle box. Rob had a seizure then and there. While Andy was waiting for him to return, two other people found him and called 911.

The emergency crew arrived and tried to revive him. They put the paddles on his chest and everything. But it didn't work, and Rob was gone. He passed from the physical plane that day, August 12, 2000.

It's amazing to me that Cathy and Rob had so much in common. They both died of head injuries, and they both loved animals. I remember one time when Rob rescued a raccoon that had been hit by a car. Rob was in the street trying to help the animal, agitated and dying. I warned him to stay away from the raccoon, fearful it might bite him, but he just wanted to save any animal. Cathy was like that, too.

Neither of them made it through high school, but both got their GEDs. It seems like such a miracle that Martha and I would come together. I joined AA-EVP in January 2001, and Martha joined in 2002. I made the connection with Martha just after my father had passed in 2002. We began sharing stories about the signs that she was getting from Cathy and the signs that I was getting from Rob, as well as the signs that tied the two of them together. There were so many similarities that we began to notice.

Then came dreams that Martha had about Cathy with a blonde-haired boy and dreams that I would have about Rob and

Cathy. Then came dreams from perfect strangers of my son and a blonde-haired girl!

Rob before the accident

One day I went to work and someone I worked with came up and said, "Karen, I need to talk to you. It's so important. I had a dream, and I have to tell you about it." So when we had a quiet moment, Judy related the story: "Karen, your son came to me in a dream last night. It's true, I've never met him, but somehow I knew it was your son. I was in a store and another woman I work with was there, and you were there. The other woman said to you, 'We have to leave right now,' and you left me alone in the store. Suddenly there was a bright light, and your son was there. I know it was him, and I know that he came to me because you weren't ready yet. He came to me with a woman, but not a woman-woman. It was a girlfriend type, who had short, blonde hair. He told me that he had found another love, and that he was okay. He said he was happy, and I needed to let you know that."

It was so profound to hear this from a person who never even knew Rob, nor anything about him or Cathy! She had never even heard a story about my friendship with Martha, yet she relates this dream! I'm still amazed at all this synchronicity.

Over the years we've had a lot of EVP communications from Rob. Martha got one that clearly said, "Cathy Browning." She was stumped by this, because she didn't know anyone by that name. Then it dawned on her: Rob's last name was Browning. I think it's an unmistakable message that they're together on the Other Side.

When Martha and I talked about this, I said, "Oh, my God! Do you think they got married? They didn't even tell us!" Then we decided that it was a simplification, that Cathy had used this as a way of telling her that both of them were there at the time of this message. It's not significant to think about 'marriage' on the Other Side, not the way we know it here. Rather I think it indicates the involvement they both have in The Big Circle.

It seems Cathy is a ringleader on the Other Side. She has sent such large volumes of EVP to Martha, and the communication is so strong. Part of the reason might be that Cathy was studying these topics before she crossed over. I think this might be one reason her communication is so strong. Now Martha has started the recording group, Bridge to the Afterlife. And what Martha and I have done, along with help from those on the Other Side, is to form a spiritual connection, a true bridge to our kids on the Other Side. Interestingly, more and more get added to the roster every day, those trying to bridge the gap, to speak through the veil, and to communicate with us here. They want to speak to their own loved ones, and we provide a connection on this side to begin to accomplish that. We form part of The Big Circle, and those on the Other Side form part of The Big Circle, and it's almost just a technical thing. They communicate with us because we're listening, but they most want to get messages to those they love.

There's a remarkable story that I just posted online at the AA-EVP site. Another woman responded telling me that it was wonderful that we were receiving messages from the Other Side, and to remember that I am merely a conduit for this to happen. Martha is a similar conduit with a very large capacity to receive the energy of those on the Other Side.

As an example of this, Martha received an EVP in Georgia that listed many of the names in The Big Circle. My exact voice was in it! And I'm here in New Hampshire. You could hear Cathy's voice saying, *"Spirit room. Test, test."* Then **my** voice said **my** name. Other members of the group were stunned by this, wondering how in the heck that could happen. I don't know how my voice ended up there. I'm certainly here in the physical plane. Perhaps I astrally projected myself to Georgia as part of The Big Circle. And after my voice, there was Rob's voice saying, as clear as could be, *"Yep, this is Rob."* It was incredible.

My father, who passed more recently, was a spiritual man, and he and I have always had a special bond. Before he passed, he knew about my communications with Rob. One of the most interesting things here is that I can smell my father when he's around me, just as I can smell Rob when he's around. My dad wore Old Spice, which nobody wears anymore. So when I smell Old Spice in my house, I know Dad's around. I'll just open up my arms and say, "I can't see you Dad, but I know you're here. I'm opening my arms to give you a great big hug." And I know he's hugging me back. Sometimes I'll be driving down the highway with my two boys, and we'll suddenly smell cigarette smoke. Rob smoked. We'll all look at each other and say, "Do you smell that?" and we'll laugh. He's there.

A medium once told me that Rob and I had experienced many lifetimes together and that he was a very advanced soul. He knew for a long time that he wouldn't live very long in this lifetime. I'd pester him about quitting smoking, and he'd say, "What's the difference, Mom? I'm not going to live very long." Of course, that's something a mother never wants to hear. I'd say, "Stop it! Don't say that!" But he always knew. He knew the day before he passed that he would have a seizure.

One day I was outside raking leaves in the front yard, and I stopped suddenly as my eyes welled up with tears. I said, "I know you're right in front of me, Rob. You're right here. I know you're right here." I could feel him there, just as I felt his presence when he was alive. This occurrence is not unique to me. Many people report knowing when their deceased loved ones are present. Martha knows when Cathy is there. She just knows it. I can't describe the feeling; it's like I've suddenly stepped into another dimension. As it happens, I'm in a daze. I might even feel someone brush right by me. This is my comfort. I need to go through the rest of my life knowing that I'm not alone, that in addition to my kids who are still alive, Rob and my dad are still here. They're helping me walk through this life that I must finish.

Recently, three of my daughter's friends have passed, one after the other. It was a horrible month. One of the friends who passed over was named Adam DuBowik, twenty-three. He tragically and accidentally overdosed on recreational drugs, substances he got from someone he thought was his friend.

My son, Alex, is thirteen years old, and one of his best friends is Ben DuBowik, also thirteen. Ben is Adam's brother. Like many of Alex's friends, Ben had shown an interest in EVP. Many of these boys ask me to record something when they come over; they just seem to love the technology and the possibilities.

After Adam passed, it was some time (probably three weeks) before Ben came over again. When I saw him, I said, "Ben, I want you to know that Alex and I know that Adam died. We've walked a similar path with the loss of Rob. Please know that we're here for you and your mom if you need us, because we understand how difficult this can be."

Later that evening, Ben asked if I would record an EVP to contact Adam. Alex, Ben, and I sat down together. I turned on the recorder and called out for those in The Big Circle to see if they could find Adam and to tell Adam that we are sending messages of love. We requested that he send a message to us if he could. That's all we said. When we played back the recorder, we heard silence, then *"**Ben, I love you... I'll be back**."* Ben's eyes filled up. He said, "That's my brother's voice!"

Karen wrote this letter to Mrs. DuBowik:

My name is Karen Mossey, and I'm a member of AA-EVP (www.aaevp.com), and a specialist in EVP (Electronic Voice Phenomena). My son Alex and Ben are very good friends, and my daughter Jessica Browning was good friends with Adam. My son Rob Browning passed to spirit in 2000 and my father in 2002. I have received more comfort and help in my grieving process through the work I do. I know from EVP that life continues. We have formed a spiritual circle, Bridge to the Afterlife, with our children on the Other Side. I hope it is OK that I have added Adam's name to my roster for prayers and meditation.

Ben had an interesting EVP after Adam's passing. He thought it would be okay to share the message we received last night after we asked those in spirit to help us reach out to Adam and send love. We recorded the message below. Ben says that it is Adam's voice. We heard him say, **"Ben... I love you... I'll be back."**

I hope this message is okay to share with you. If not, I understand. **But I do believe** *that Adam is in a good place, that he is okay. My prayers are for your comfort.*

~ Karen Mossey, Alex's Mother.

Ben later asked me if I would send the clip to his parents, telling me they truly wanted to hear it, so I did. Soon after I took Alex and Ben to the movies. When I dropped him off that night, Ben's mother Judy came to me and hugged me. We talked for an hour, and we cried together. She said, "You've given me the message that I needed. You've let me know that my son is okay. You've helped me so much, brought me so much comfort." I told her that she could call me any time, and that I'd come sit with her. She told me how happy she was that we had added Adam's name to our roster. She told me that she listened to the clip over and over. At one point, she wandered into the other room and when she heard his voice on the recording, she ran back in, exclaiming, "It's him! I know it's him!"

Of Jessie's friends who have died, it's interesting that Adam is the only one we have contacted. I know this is because I had a connection to him through Ben. Jessie knew Jonathan, Blair and Brian, but I didn't know them. Ben and Alex have been friends for years, and Ben had always wanted to do EVP when he came over. I had already told him stories of my son Rob, who was in the spirit world. I had explained that I do what I do because there is no death; it's just a transition, a change that we go through. But your personality, your soul, your spirit survives. I told him I know this because I've heard my son's voice and my father's voice.

In fact, I sent a clip of my father's voice to Tom and Lisa Butler, and they played it on a television interview they did. People who knew my father heard it and emailed me saying, "Karen, it's Stanley! It's his voice exactly!" There is so much evidence out there, and the sense of connection among us, Cathy, Rob and Braden. And Cathy is connected to everyone, because she's the ringleader, it's too much to be just meaningless coincidence. It's real.

This was evident when we called out for Adam, asking for the help of The Big Circle in contacting him. A soft, feminine voice spoke just before his voice and said, ***"Ben..."*** but I haven't made out who it was. I always ask The Big Circle, those in spirit, to help me when I try to make contact. I seriously believe that the energy of all of those who were in the room that night also allowed Adam to come through.

Now someone might ask what I mean by the term "spiritual." For me, people are very spiritual when they believe strongly in the afterlife. They embrace spirituality, other dimensions, and higher levels, the spirit. It's not a person who's a ghost-hunter, although some spiritual people may do this. But spiritual people are comfortable in themselves, in knowing that life continues and that everything and all of us are connected. Spirituality extends to others, in kindness and goodness toward others. It continues as our soul continues. To know what's inside of us, to live from our soul, to understand that we are eternal beings; all this constitutes spirituality for me.

I love the interconnectedness of all of this. I love to tell the story about a dream Martha had about Cathy and Rob at a fishing cottage. What's amazing to me is that the cottage she described is actually a birdhouse in my home. When I sent Martha the picture of this, she was astounded at the connection. She also had a dream in which Rob was telling Cathy that his mom was a very good artist. In fact, I am a painter, which Martha would have had no way of knowing prior to this dream. I began to have repeated visions of Rob and Cathy dancing, and I felt I needed to paint this. It was interesting, because although Martha and Cathy both loved dancing, Rob was not very fond of it. In another dream that Martha had later, Cathy told Martha that Rob had sent to me the vision of them dancing so that she would know that he is happy.

Meanwhile, Martha decided to send me a wooden artist's studio box. She knew it was somewhere in the house and spent quite some time looking for it. Martha had looked repeatedly in Cathy's room but could not find the box. She told me, "I kept hearing Cathy's voice in my head telling me to look in her room, just one more time." When she finally heeded the message, there was the artist's set, sitting in the middle of Cathy's bed. She said, "I guess Cathy wanted the box sent to Karen, too."

I'm amazed day after day at the messages we've received from our kids about things that neither of us had ever known. It has helped Martha and us to truly bond, and our kids seem to have had quite a hand in this from the Other Side. And we've found that the more we acknowledge the signs from the Other Side, the more they are sent. Too often we are just running through life without any time to stop and smell the roses. Spiritual moments like this occur when we slow down and take the time to commune, to see the butterflies, to observe the red cardinal or white dove flying overhead as you're thinking about your child. When one acknowledges this as a sign, it's part of becoming spiritual.

Losing a child is so horrific, the worst pain anyone could possibly suffer. And I hesitate to use the word "lose," because Rob is not "lost." Although I cannot see him, I know he sees me. I haven't truly lost him, but I can't hold him anymore. And our relationship, although it continues, has changed. Yet it does continue. Part of who I am is my son, and he has integrated parts of me. Holding the horrible grief of this transition has helped me to understand all these things. It's strange that it takes a tragedy like this to get us to slow down and begin to really communicate with what's happening around us. I have a different outlook on life now. I really do. My eyes have opened a bit wider through these beautiful things that have happened.

~ Karen Mossey

Vicki Talbott and Braden—and Jim

Braden Talbott Lindholdt

Vicki Talbott sent this story via email:

My son Braden and his friend Jim died March 11, 2001, during a kayak outing on Puget Sound. While the kayaks were discovered the next morning, the boys' bodies were never found. Braden and Jim were best friends and both were twenty years old. Both had an interest in the afterlife and various aspects of spirit communication, including spirit photography and Electronic Voice Phenomena (EVP). About five months after they died, they started manifesting in photos, which various family members have taken. They both left messages on my answering machine as well.

*Braden left a number of messages, including **"Whaddup," "Mom,"** and a short rap segment. (He was a musician, after all, so there was no mistaking it was him.) Jim left one saying, **"Mom, I'll come again,"** and left it when his mother was visiting me. These were clearly verifiable as the boy's voices were identical to their living voices.*

In early 2004, I felt drawn to AA-EVP. I had visited the website many times in years prior, but never felt the need to join until then. Surprisingly, Braden and Cathy, Martha's daughter, seemed to have a hand in several mothers finding and joining the group. I had read about Rob and Cathy, the children of Karen and Martha, and thought it highly likely that Braden knew them. After introducing myself to the group, someone remembered that before I had joined and during one of the Bridge to the Afterlife sessions, someone came through on a EVP saying, **"It's Brad-n."**

We were all excited to feel confirmation in the form of the EVP before I had even joined! This seemed to illustrate Braden's presence in the group on the Other Side, which I had sensed. Since then, Braden and Jim have come through many times, often with Cathy and other members of The Big Circle, but sometimes by themselves, just stopping by to say **"love you."** *Braden*

Braden's friend, Jim

and Cathy have come through in moments of hilarity, with Braden asking Cathy to help him sing, starting with Cathy heralding Braden's presence with **"Braden's here,"** *and Braden saying* **"Hi!"** *Then conversation between Cathy and Braden will ensue with such comments as* **"Let's sing it again, Cathy!"** *and* **"Don't you sing so sexy!"**

I can tell you that both mothers of these young men are forever grateful for communication from the boys and from everyone else in The Big Circle. We look forward to EVP helping others from both sides in their adjustment process after suffering the difficult physical separation from loved ones. ~ Vicki

I sent this in return:

> *Not long after I received this in my inbox, I did some EVP recording in Cathy's room. I happened to ask if she was with anyone from The Big Circle, and near the end of the recording, I can clearly hear her voice say, "**Braden.**" ~ Martha*

On March 4, 2004, members of the Recording Circle were sharing their collected EVP. I was recording in Cathy's bedroom, and I got a young man's voice saying "Angel," followed by "Everybody heard me there." Cheri, a member of our Recording Circle, edited the clip for me, and when we asked around about who it might be, we got the following email messages from Vicki:

> *In this clip, I think I hear two voices. One says "**Angel,**" then the other says "**Everybody heard me there.**" The second one really sounds like Braden! He was a rap artist! Does anyone else think it sounds like their loved one before I get too excited?*
>
> *~ Vicki*

> *Hi, all – I'm referring to the [EVP] "**Angel... Everybody heard me there**" clip. As you can see from my earlier comments, I was astounded by how much it sounded like my son Braden. Last night one of his good friends came over for a visit. I played her a couple of the EVP that I had gotten of women's voices, then I played the "**Everybody...**" clip without prefacing what she would be hearing. Well, she immediately burst into tears, exclaiming, "That's Braden!" I just thought I'd let you all know!*
>
> *~ Vicki*

A beautiful part of belonging to the AA-EVP is that we are able to share our EVP clips with people all over the world who are connected through this organization. We have members who are very talented at editing the recordings. Sometimes when I send a clip into the group, another member will work on it. When they send it back to me, they've been able to pull out more voices than I could discern in my own process.

More from Karen and Rob

Karen sent this some time ago:

I remembered something last night Martha: When Rob first transitioned in 2000, I went to see April Sheerin. She is a very good medium, and also now the minister of the Spiritualist church I attend. I wanted so much to hear from Rob. She gave me the most profound messages from him, with evidence only he could have given to her.

She knew nothing about me at the time I first saw her. One of the things she did tell me was that Rob would begin to come through very strongly within the period between three and five years after his passing. But that at this point he was being held back from me because he had things to learn and because I was not ready. At first this upset me, because I wanted to hear from him so much, right then.

Now as I have come to the fourth year after he crossed over, I am stunned at this revelation. I see how far I have come in these years, and how much more prepared I am now for his messages. I believe that he is now settled and ready as well to send messages through. We now have both matured spiritually enough to open up a line of communication.

Rob sent the name Marvin through you, as a strong clue to me that this was a message from him. Cathy and Rob know they can send this through either of us because we are close, and we both will understand. This is all part of their plan, a bigger plan, part of which was our meeting each other. It is important that messages that we feel may have significance to anyone in The Big Circle be sent to the group. The message may not personally be for the one receiving it, but you can bet it's meant for someone in the group.

Their awareness of the total is greater then ours. They see beyond what our physical eyes see. Rob and Cathy know we are "figuring it out." But here on the physical we are a bit more "dense" (no pun intended, but it's true, we are), and things take us longer.

Love, Karen

Karen "In" the Spirit Room

Karen has already written about this incident from her viewpoint. Here is the account, which I recorded in late June 2004. We conducted our usual Recording Circle session at the appointed time. I entered the Spirit Room with my recorder. When I emerged, I listened to the tape, found a considerable amount of EVP and reported the following:

> *"Hey, Cat"* (male EVP)
> *"It's your mother"* (male EVP)
> *"Sir, sir"* (Cathy's voice)
> *"Karen"* (female EVP)
> *"Pray for me"* (Cathy's voice)
> *"Mom"* (Cathy)
> *"You never got a chance, huh?"* (female EVP)

To me, the voice that said *"Karen"* sounded exactly like the voice of Karen Mossey. When I sent the clips to her, she responded that at the end she thought she heard, *"This is Rob."* She continued:

> *How happy I am! Do you think Rob was sending me a message, and used my name instead of Mom to let me know he was there? I feel so comforted.*
>
> Love, Kare

Vicki Talbott responded:

> Kare ~ I thought I heard that, too! I also hear Braden saying, **"Hi, Cathy,"** which I clipped and sent over to Martha to listen to. Yea, Rob! I'll bet it was him saying, **"Karen."** Braden has used my name in the past.
>
> Love, Vicki

Karen listened to the clip a bit more, admitting that this did sound exactly like her voice. She emailed us back with this realization, adding:

> Do you think Rob may have possibly duplicated my exact voice pattern to get me a message? And this brings up a point: Has anyone ever experienced spirit duplicating an exact voice pattern? I know I wasn't in Martha's Spirit Room that night, but that is definitely my voice...   Kare

Kathy Malone and Lance

Lance Malone

I remember when I first met Kathy. She came into my house wearing a baseball cap and an old pair of jeans. She was adorable, like a beloved cartoon character out of Charlie Brown. Yes, you guessed it: Peppermint Patty! Beneath that baseball cap I found a very smart woman with a heart of gold. Actually, all the ladies that meet at my house for our recording sessions are truly wonderful, brave, and strong women.

Kathy emailed this story:

My son Lance was killed May 29, 1995, at the age of twenty-five, on his motorcycle. Before that, I had certainly known some desperate grief. My son Scott died at only sixteen hours old in 1971, and my yet-unborn daughter Erin was miscarried in the spring of 1974.

I came to know about EVP and Martha through my friend Judy. Wanting very much to have contact, not only with Lance, but my other two children Scott and Erin. I went with my friend Judy to Martha's home for a "Bridge To The Afterlife" meditation and recording session. This was my first try at contacting my children, and I was never very good at meditating, so I really didn't expect to have any contact. Martha put me in a room by myself and told me what to do. During our recording time, I asked Lance some very general questions that required only "yes" or "no" answers. "Is it okay to contact you? Are you okay? Can you hear me?"

When the recording session was over, Martha was kind enough to take the time and go through what each of us had recorded. To my surprise, while listening to the play-back, I heard Lance's voice. I was so amazed. This was not just a voice; it was clearly Lance's! I was so shocked! It took me a couple of seconds before I could ask Martha to go back so we could listen to it again, and again I heard the same thing. I asked everyone else to listen and tell me what they heard. I didn't tell the others what I had heard after listening to the recording a few times, but they all came up with the same thing. Of course, they had no way of knowing that in fact it was Lance's voice but just hearing the words made me realize that this was possible. We all heard, **"Mom, I'm here."**

I have been recording now for almost a year, and have had about four contacts from Lance. I believe that in time we may have more, but I feel that both Lance and I are new at this and have much to learn. Lance was not a talker here on earth, so I expect nothing more now. And anything that I get is a true gift from him. I hope in time he will teach Scott and Erin to come through.

Love, Kathy

Now that Kathy has told her story, I have one: When I was showing my niece Rachel the memorial web page that has the photos of our loved ones, she saw Lance's picture, and she freaked. Rachel had been telling me about a recurring dream she was having where Cathy is with this boy at what appears to be an airport. In her dream, Cathy and this boy are helping the new arrivals into the spirit world. Cathy and Lance are much like a welcoming committee, and Cathy tells Rachel this is her job. Rachel looked at the photo, her eyes flashed wide, and she said, "Oh my God! This is the same boy that I have seen in that airport dream with Cathy!" We smiled at the synchronicities, at how The Big Circle just keeps growing, both here and on the Other Side.

Bea Hofman and Lauren

Lauren Thompson

Bea Hofman contacted me after the death of her daughter Lauren. I emailed to her the following message:

Dear Beatrice,

We know our children have not gone away; they simply exist at a different vibration than ours. Death is not an end, just the next stage of life. Keep this thought, and do not let anyone prevent you from trying to establish contact with your daughter. Remember that you do this out of love and concern. People try to tell me that by contacting Cathy I am holding her back. However, our contacts are a mutual exchange. How can we hold them back? Do we have such power? Did we have the power to prevent their deaths?

The mothers of our group have all had successful contacts with their deceased children. We feel that our children are together in what Cathy (my now-deceased daughter) has called

The Big Circle. Lauren's story is similar to Cathy's. Cathy also suffered from depression at the time of her death, and she too was very intelligent and gifted. Cathy was killed in an automobile accident, but she knew her time was up before that accident.

Other bereaved mothers and I do a bi-weekly recording session which we call Recording Circle - Bridge to the Afterlife. The group, most of whom I met at Compassionate Friends, meets at my home every other Thursday at 8:00 P.M. EST. Then we connect with others online who have asked for contact at the same time. You are invited to join us from wherever you are. When you record, simply ask for Lauren, or ask someone from The Big Circle to come through for you.

Please feel free to introduce yourself to the mothers of the Recording Circle - Bridge to the Afterlife group before the next session. You will find them very supportive. If you use the [AA-EVP] e-group, please tell your story using the title "Recording Circle - Bridge to the Afterlife." You may also display your message in the "Idea Exchange Discussion Board" under the "Recording Circle - Bridge to the Afterlife" heading. Of course, any action you take is up to you.

Best Regards, Martha

Here is Bea's story, sent via email:

Lauren was a student at Johns Hopkins University. While there, she took on an internship at the Baltimore Zoo teaching gifted and talented children. She had just completed her sophomore year. Lauren was also on the swim team. The memories I have of my daughter are of pure love. She loved the world and never judged. I believe her purpose here was to teach all that met her to live with unconditional love.

Lauren was brilliant and talented beyond comprehension. She never wanted any praise. Once when she was eight years old she told me, "Mom, Aunt Jean dotes on me too much." Her work ethic was unreal, and her coaches all commented on her efforts.

In what might have been a moment of despair, Lauren went to the roof of the building where she resided and called for help. Two friends were there and commented to her that what she was doing was not funny. They thought she was kidding. She started coming back from the edge of the roof when her foot slipped and she fell. I know that Lauren was in despair at the time she went to the roof because she was seeing a counselor after she had started feeling depressed. She had no idea what was causing the depression, nor did I.

I do know that three weeks before her death I saw a review of her life, and thought, "Why am I seeing this?" I actually thought this was crazy, because at no time did I ever think my daughter was in any danger of losing her life.

After her funeral I talked with one of her roommates, and she told me that Lauren said she did not want to die, but felt that she did not belong here. I believe with all my heart that Lauren was not supposed to be on earth after June 24, 2004. Her freak accident was what I call "predestined." I know that Lauren was supposed to leave this dimension. You see, I believe that there are Angels among us.

When I received the phone call at 5:00 A.M. telling me that my daughter was in the hospital, and what had happened, I knew she would not make it. I did not know the extent of her injuries; I knew that she was already with me. I didn't get crazy or upset. I just accepted it. It wasn't until the missing her kicked in that I became sad. I talked to her every day then, and I still talk to her everyday. I stay away from people who pity me and act as if she is not here.

I suffered and still suffer the death of my daughter. It was only at the time of death that I seemed to be in acceptance. After the missing kicked in, I was in complete agony. I still have moments of despair, and who knows when these will end.

I feel Lauren is somewhere, but because of the Laws of Nature and our lack of science and research, I cannot communicate with her in the old ways. I first read Mark Macy's "Miracle in the Storm" when I realized that there was a possibility of me communicating with my daughter again. Since then I've read Sarah Estep's "Voices of Eternity." This is what brought me to become a member of the AA-EVP group.

*I started recording June 28, 2004. On July 8, 2004, I recorded a message saying, **"Hi, hi!"** from a voice that sounded exactly like my grandmother. I have not had any more voices re-*

corded since that time, but I am still recording. I know that I will get other communications. I have also had several dreams that have given me messages about Lauren. I plan to join the group of moms that are trying to communicate with their children.

Thanks for writing this book. I do believe that collective consciousness will help us communicate.

Love, Bea Hofman (Lauren's Mom)

Siobhan and Tony

Anthony (Tony) James Sexton

Siobhan McBride sent a long and beautiful story about how her son Tony's conception, birth and life had been very different from her other sons. Throughout most of his life, Tony preferred spending lots of time with his mom, being involved in most things she was interested in. She said, "We used to watch *Sightings* and *The Extraordinary* TV shows together and play little psychic card games together, trying to guess what card we'd draw from the stack." She was surprised when he turned sixteen and began working and driving and behaving much more independently than he had in earlier years. He also developed friendships with people she didn't know.

Her story continues:

> On Saturday May 26th, he was going out to a youth club with these new friends. Before he was to go, I told him I still owed him a birthday dinner, and asked him to go to get som*e Chinese food with his little brother and me. We had our last dinner to-*

gether. That evening he stayed out all night, arriving home in the early morning. He slept for awhile, then got ready to go to a drum circle as he had planned.

I was planning to take his little brother to the movies. As I was getting ready in the bathroom, Tony called out to me that he was leaving. Normally, I would have gone to him and given him a hug and a kiss, and said, "Be safe, I love you." This time I just said, "Bye, honey," and stayed in the bathroom. I felt paralyzed, just frozen, like I couldn't go to him. I thought to myself, "What is the matter with you?" but I couldn't do anything. After I heard the door slam, I was able to finish getting ready. For some reason, I felt extremely tired. I just wanted to lie down and go to sleep. It was only 1:00 P.M., so I had no reason to feel that way.

After the movie, my youngest son and I walked around the mall for a little while, then left to go home. As we got on the freeway, I had to swerve to miss another car. Then about a mile down the road, I commented that I smelled funeral flowers. There was a strong floral fragrance that just came into the car for a split second.

That evening about 8:00 P.M., two highway patrolmen came to the door to say Tony had been killed in a car accident. The report listed his time of death as 4:51 P.M. The car in which he was traveling was in the same lane that I was when I smelled the funeral flowers, except that I was about thirty miles south of where his accident had happened.

While I have never had an actual visitation from Tony, in the sense of seen an apparition or anything, I have had telepathic communication, as well as audible communication. The night after he died, when I was turning off our swamp cooler, as the blades were winding down, I heard his voice coming through. It was right after I had said, "I always feel your presence when I am in the hall." I couldn't understand what he was saying because it seemed like trying to tune in an old radio, when it doesn't quite get onto the station, but it was his voice.

Another thing that has happened was this: I telepathically received a message to take a purple crystal heart to the girl who held him while he died. She was in the front seat and miraculously survived the accident. The boy driving had also been

*killed. I telepathically said back to the thought, "I don't think I
have one of those," but went to look anyway. (I used to have a
gift shop and had some items left from it.) Sure enough, when I
opened the door to the storage room, an amethyst heart was the
very first thing that caught my eye.*

*Tony's friends have had numerous communications and visi-
tations from him. One of my older sons was having a very difficult time with his grief. He actually saw Tony standing in our
home in the middle of the day. I know that if he could only use a
certain amount of his energy to appear to one of us, this particular brother of Tony's needed it the most.*

*A friend of mine told me about EVP, and we attempted it a
couple of times. We didn't get anything. Then he told me about
the AA-EVP group he had heard about on the Coast to Coast AM
radio show. I immediately joined. I told a co-worker of mine
about it, and she also joined. She was an avid ghost-hunter already. One evening my co-worker and her sister were at the
cemetery where Tony is buried. They asked him if he had anything he'd like to say to me, and they recorded an EVP of him
saying,* **"She's doing a good job."** *They also got a photo with
several orbs in it, one of which looks very much like Tony's
head.*

*On another occasion, I was at the cemetery and got a re-
cording saying,* **"Foona's here."** *Foona was a nickname I had
given to Tony because he was a Pisces. It was a shortened version of "tuna fish."*

*There are many instances when 1 have felt his presence, es-
pecially through songs on the radio. I am looking forward to col-
lecting more EVP as I learn more about how it is done. Martha
is a wonderful support person and she has helped more people
than anyone could ever know.*

*Looking back on Tony's life, I have felt like he knew he
wouldn't be here long. He lived his life very quickly and fully. At
the funeral home, while making arrangements for his burial, the
funeral director asked me, "Did he just graduate?" I thought for
a minute, because it hadn't dawned on me until then that if he
had stayed in public school, he would have just been graduating
that week. Instead he accomplished much more, things that*

would have been more in keeping with someone in their mid-twenties.

I have been a local facilitator for The Compassionate Friends, and I think having discussion about communications with our children on the Other Side is of utmost importance in healing.

~ Siobhan K. McBride

Unique Friendships Form

Mia's Grave

Our group has joined together people from all over the world, and although we have not had the opportunity to meet in person, we have formed wonderful and unique friendships through emails.

Peter Mikkelsen resides in Denmark and has not only made friends with an AA-EVP member, Andrea Carr, but also a young girl who is in spirit named Mia. Below is Peter's story.

Mia

It began with something, which even today, I cannot explain. When something really terrible and tragic happens and you hear about it in the news, or read about it, you react immediately with shock and think how horrible it is. After a time, this dies away and life moves on. One reason for this is there are so many things in your daily life, and this tragedy gets pushed into the background. That did not happen to me last summer [2003] when a truly sweet twelve-year-old girl, Mia was killed over here [in Denmark]. My reaction was just the opposite.

I won't give you details about the murder, as they are so horrible and shocking that the entire country was seriously disturbed by it. Lots of people went to the scene of the crime, and later to the cemetery, to place flowers and show their respect. I, too, went to the cemetery and paid my respects to the poor girl. I even took a couple of pictures of her grave that was covered with flowers and stuffed animals. I could not forget her, and how she was killed and how her young killer could do such a terrible thing. It was as if I had known her, whom I did not, and her tragic ending haunted me.

Something inside me kept urging me to reach out and help this child find peace. Instinctively, I placed a small photo of her beside my microphone and started trying to contact Mia by the use of EVP. In my recordings I picked up a girl's sounds: a sigh; a clearing sound of the throat, heartbeats, even a line of sounds not too far apart including a soft blow into the mike, a rustling sound close to the mike and then the sound of pages on a small pad being turned over; everything except a voice.

One day, as I was trying to concentrate on her, I felt a slight cold breeze across my face. However, I do realize that all these occurrences may not be related to Mia, but there have been many signs that I just have not been able to rule out as not being her. Some of these signs have been in the form of knocking or tapping noises, and there have been many.

Perhaps since Mia was a child, I associated her with Eric Clapton's touching song, *Tears in Heaven.* Last winter, there was a period where the recording for EVP seemed to not have anything of value, and I began to think to myself, "Why don't you just give up?"

How do I know she would even send me signs? Just at the precise moment I turned on the radio, and the song, *Tears in Heaven* began to play.

One of my friends wrote, "I think you have a connection to that little girl." God works in mysterious ways, and maybe you are the agent to help bring her to peace."

At that point my friend, Andrea Carr, who has given me so much help and support, told my story to a mediumistic friend. Her friend verified that Mia indeed still was earthbound,* and she told me how I could help her move onwards into the Spiritual World. Apparently, I did manage, through prayers and meditation, to direct her on, as she should.

In private emails to Martha Copeland, I explained my story and sent her a photo of Mia to add to the AA-EVP Memorial Website, and include her name on the Spiritual Roster.

Martha told me this: "I looked at Mia's picture this morning and I felt she was surrounded in a wonderful light of love and friendship. You and Mia are a team. This pact, or team, was a decision you both agreed upon before entering the physical plane. You and Mia have been together in many different lifetimes, but on this particular life journey you had different lessons to learn, and chose to be apart. This is the reason you feel such a strong connection to Mia. It does not matter that you did not physically know Mia during her brief life; your friendships were formed in Heaven creating a strong bond between the two of you.

"Spirit comes to us in all sorts of ways and what you have described in your emails is just a few. Having Mia's picture close by will draw her around you, and remember, 'Thoughts are things.' If you are praying, and thinking about Mia you are creating an 'energy thought form' in the spiritual world that she will be able to pick up on. Our thoughts, when received in the spiritual, world can be compared to the likeness of a lighthouse. We are projecting our thought forms into the spiritual world in the same way a lighthouse shines a beam of light into the sky. However, the difference is that your beam of light shining into the spiritual world has your energy attached to it. This is how spirit can recognize who is trying to contact them from the physical world.

"Try to keep a journal of all the 'subtle' spirit contacts that you receive on a daily basis. This increases your awareness of your own spiritual growth along with strengthening your own ability in contacting Mia. Before going to sleep, tell yourself you will remember your dreams and ask Mia to come to you in your dreams. Take baby steps when working with spirit—it is good that you have chosen the AA-EVP group to help you in your spiritual journey."

My story of Mia is a long story, and of course a very moving one for me. I am eternally grateful for those who have advised me about how to help Mia, and I hope that I will get a closer contact with her, and I have no doubt that I will meet her one day, when I pass on, our friendship will continue in Heaven.

I asked Martha if she would try to contact Mia and she asked that I please not confuse her with the famous medium, John Edward, because she could not achieve results like he does. She further explained that the wonderful thing about EVP is that it allows you to contact your loved ones without the service of a so called "middleman," such as a psychic or medium. It is the act of receiving confirmation from a loved one in the spiritual world by the use of EVP for yourself which is a truly amazing and life altering experience; thus, this begins your healing process. However, Martha said she would try to contact Mia with her recorder and on Wednesday, June 30, 2004, and we think she succeeded in her mission.

With Cathy's help, and her friends in the "Big Circle" Martha asked for Mia to please come through for us and let us know if she is happy in her new surroundings. Following Martha's voice on the recorder is the voice of a young girl answering, ***"Yes, yes, I am happy."***

I feel assured that Mia has moved on spirituality and has joined forces with the children belonging to the "Big Circle."

* A person who has "died" but who refuses to go on "to the light" is referred to as an earthbound entity. The reasons a person might become earthbound include the possibility that the person is not aware of the fact that they are no longer living in the physical, they did something "sinful" and fear judgment, they are waiting for someone to "raise them up" or they are attached to something still in the physical. It is possible to hold a loved one near with grief.

Memorial Website

Due to the increased interest of EVP generated by the educational trailer released by Universal Studios for the movie *White Noise*, we have added a website for the "Big Circle." Lisa Yesse volunteered to create the "Big Circle" website and Michael Sullivan, and Cheryl Bain, group members, have volunteered their services in helping Lisa maintain this website for our Recording Circle - Bridge to the Afterlife group.

There are many who join our bi-weekly Recording Circle - Bridge to the Afterlife sessions, we thought it might help to have available pictures of those who were on our Spiritual Roster, those for whom we are praying or with whom we were asking for communication, so a memorial web page was created. If you would like to add a loved one to this memorial website, and are a member of the AA-EVP, please send an email request to http://bigcircle.aaevp.com and the photograph you would like to have posted, along with the person's full name, date of birth and death, and any short memorial message you would like to have included

We are most grateful to our members who have provided us with this service. It's so beautiful to view the faces of the names on our list each Thursday when we gather. Both for those at my home, and for those scattered around the world who join us, we can feel more deeply our common bonds when we are all viewing the loved ones of those in our group.

AA-EVP Technical Gurus

Our group is very fortunate to have people like Mike Sullivan who are the technical gurus for our group and are available to members experiencing any computer or technical problems.

When I first started with this group, Mike telephoned me and walked me through the "how to" for operating the Cool Edit Program, along with many other programs used for filtering EVP clips. (Yes, I received instructions when I purchased these programs, but for me, they were of no help.) Mike conducted a workshop at our conference held in Reno on teaching people how to filter their EVP clips and work with their recordings

We are lucky to have Mike, as well as other members who are willing to add their support and help for our AA-EVP group.

Tom and Lisa Butler have devoted their lives to the American Association of Electronic Phenomena (AA-EVP) and have one of the best handbooks for working with EVP entitled *There is No Death and There are No Dead*, which can be ordered by going to: www.aaevp.com or www.amazon.com.

Nothing New

I picked up a book entitled, *Childlight: How Children Reach Out to Their Parents from the Beyond,* by Donna Thiesen and Dary Matera. It's good to know that others are experiencing something like this. In the introduction, a grieving mother wrote:

> "Even though we share the same anguish, the same losses, women mainly cling together while men mostly become islands of silence. Thankfully, I've discovered that I can phone any of my new female friends who've experienced similar losses night or day, and they will drop everything and listen. I can cry, scream, yell, curse, get silly, make sick jokes and prattle on, and no one complains. Although I've met only a few of them face to face, the love and acceptance we share is hard for outsiders to imagine."

I'm not sure I can do a better job than this of describing succinctly the camaraderie which exists among our group. Although we've mostly come together to record EVP, we always share the many other ways we experience our deceased loved ones, from dreams and visions seen waking or sleeping, to voices heard anywhere from our gardens to our kitchens to our heads.

Part 3

Trying EVP for Yourself

Tool for Love

Some have written to me asking why I would use EVP to contact my deceased daughter. I tell them EVP is a tool for love. Communicating the love we have to others, whether they're here with us or on the Other Side, is a way of identifying and honoring the aspect of spirit which fills us all.

I have received some critical comments that our group, Recording Circle—Bridge to the Afterlife, has evolved into a "support group" rather than a purely intellectual investigative group. Is that a bad thing? Our group, which did indeed begin as a support group for grieving mothers, does engage in investigation (see the upcoming section on Research Methodology), but the basic purpose of our group *is* to alleviate pain, both our own and what might be experienced by our loved ones who have passed over.

George Anderson says, "There are two kinds of skeptics: those who say, 'I don't know' and those who say, 'I don't want to know.'" EVP exists for the first group. George also says in *Walking in the Garden of Souls* that he doesn't really care who makes fun of him. What he will never tolerate, however, is "attacks against the bereaved for their spiritual beliefs." He continues, "I have never seen someone lose their capacity to reason or make qualified judgments just because they lost a loved one. Being bereaved does not make someone stupid, just bereaved." I stand behind my choices with a similar fierceness.

For most in our recording group, our interest in EVP comes from some life-changing experience. The resulting challenge is mental, emotional and spiritual. There are groups all over the world who are dedicated to research, some of whom watch and collect data from our group. We have been fortunate to find that both types of groups, those dedicated to love and healing, as well as those dedicated to research, can be mutually supportive. Although it may appear that we have different goals, we are all making advances that previously were not possible, regardless of how we use this tool for love.

An Evolving Spiritual World

To further clarify our understanding of the spiritual realm, the analogy of a fan is useful. While our existence might look like an electric fan which has been turned off, the spiritual world would be more like a fan running at high speed. When the fan is on, you cannot see the blades which are apparent when it's off. Does this mean the blades do not individually exist when the fan is on?

It seems that as our world evolves and technology continues to grow, the spiritual world evolves in similar ways. I think we will have to change our old theories and concepts of the spiritual world when we think of all the young people who have crossed over, carrying amazing technical knowledge and skills with them.

Albert Einstein wisely said, "The religion of the future will be a cosmic religion. It should transcend personal God and avoid dogma and theology. Covering both the natural and the spiritual, it should be based on a religious sense arising from the experience of all things natural and spiritual as a meaningful unity." This sense of "meaningful unity" is beginning to unfold for many of us.

I wonder if in the future psychics will be thought of in the same way we now view travel agents, as a dying breed. Some may still seek the skills of a psychic, but many will prefer to accomplish contact to the spirit world on their own. I know I've become my own "travel agent," both in traveling this world, and the world beyond!

Cathy and the others in The Big Circle seem to have been assigned tasks related to helping us realize our full potential for making contact. We know that we humans use a very small percentage of our brains in day-to-day life. Even our knowledge of the body-mind is limited. It is not by chance that we have come together to investigate these possibilities. We are being given various pieces of the spiritual puzzle.

George Anderson speaks of various universities that have tested the "accuracy" of his work. He says that they can only "verify" ninety percent accuracy. He laughs at this because he says that those in spirit will never reveal more than that to us. In his three decades of communicating with the Other Side, he has learned that, while souls are happy to share with us things they've learned, we are here on this plane to learn our own lessons in our own ways. This is why we gather together to work with EVP. It brings more and more puzzle pieces together.

Cathy's Role

Cathy Christmas 2000

It's interesting now for me to reflect on Cathy's life and observe how keen her curiosity for the paranormal had been. The year before Cathy died, she and Rachel had purchased recorders and had begun attending meetings of a "ghost club," intent on doing their own ghost investigations. They had at times used Cathy's Ouija board. Considering the books on communicating with souls which I found in Cathy's room, I now wonder if perhaps she had already established contacts on the Other Side when she crossed over. Perhaps she was aware of The Big Circle on the Other Side even before she took her place there.

I am certain that Cathy did indeed complete her mission here. Now it seems that her mission in the spirit world is to help open the veil between that world and ours. She seems to be doing quite well with that task, too.

A number of people have asked me whether I am impeding Cathy's "progress" as a soul, wondering whether I'm keeping her "earthbound" by continuing to communicate with her. I can understand their concern and have reconciled this issue for myself.

There is a vast difference in continuing to hold on to a loved one and trying to establish a new, supportive, spiritual relationship with a loved one. In his book *Walking in the Garden of Souls*, George Anderson reminds us that it's not even possible for a soul to be held back.

We're arrogant if we believe it's even possible to do so. He also believes that "souls communicate for a variety of reasons, but the most important reason by far is because they *want* to. They want to help us understand … that we are all on a road which will eventually take us back to them."

It is true that grief-inflicted blindness may create temporary behavior of what appears to be selfishness. On the other hand, it would be impossible for contact to occur if both parties were not willing. While contact does comfort the grieving ones, it also can aid and support the growth of both those left here and those in the spiritual realm.

In a church newsletter, I circled a quotation about Plato which alludes to this bridge, echoing the same idea as Einstein expressed: "He taught that there are no contradictions, nor separations between the natural and supernatural worlds, and that man has his feet in both worlds." To many of us, this idea brings tremendous fear and anxiety about a world we cannot see or touch. I can understand this hesitation, but I haven't let it stop me.

Through our recording process, Cathy has thanked me directly for making contact. At times, she has also let me know when she was busy. You may remember that in our session with him, George Anderson provided this affirmation, stating that Cathy was happy where she was, but was also happy that we are contacting her spiritually. So even if it were possible to "hold back" a soul, this is neither my intent nor what I seem to have achieved. If Cathy's messages cease, I may have reason to question this view which seems perfect to me for now. But presently I am at peace with this practice, and it seems that Cathy is, too.

Research Methodology

People sometimes ask me about the *science* of EVP, the *proofs* of its validity. It is interesting to me that science in general tends to ask its questions from a dispassionate viewpoint; it is simply curious about what can and cannot be proven. Conversely, those who ask me about the science of EVP are often just looking to make a judgment from their own (often limited) perspective without any scientific curiosity whatsoever. So when I get these questions, I usually have a response which falls into a couple of categories, depending upon the inquiry.

I know for myself that I have begun my own "research" because I cared so much about contacting my daughter, and because I was willing to experiment with the possibilities. If I have a research question, perhaps it is this: "How does EVP help me accomplish what no other method can do?" My research is ongoing.

There are two basic kinds of scientific research: quantitative and qualitative. Science, as we've known it, usually relies on the former, because it's easier and tidier, and in many cases, prone to researcher bias. Some people think that unless an activity produces statistics, it's not science. However, in recent decades, we've learned that qualitative research, the kind that tells a story, is truly more representative of human life. It honors the belief that something which happens once is not a "fluke." Rather it is an example of what can happen within human experience, a glimpse of what is possible.

George Anderson reminds us that "part of our existence here is to live with some circumstances that the heart must understand even though they are illogical to the mind." So my heart guides me toward this experiment.

Experience matters. Anecdotes are indicators. Life itself provides data every day, whether or not we're observing it. Daily data begin to provide proofs of possibility. A favorite teacher, a world-famous MD, tells the doctors in his class, "No one is a statistic." I believe this, and I have learned that no single experience tells me anything definitive about the next experience. When I record EVP, I'm never sure exactly what will happen. I believe it is my *openness* in this process that allows me to continue to gather the data of experience which constitutes scientific inquiry. Here are some things I have learned in my ongoing experiment with EVP:

- Inquiry is *the thing*. My experiment is perhaps a long one. I have no goals for publishing my data anytime soon. Rather, I let each experience lead me to the next one, and I just continue to collect the stories which add up to my conclusions. Even those conclusions might change over time if I maintain the curiosity that allows my experiment to proceed.

- Recording devices vary in their effectiveness. Although any recording device can be used, some will work better in certain situations. I've found that it's a good idea to dedicate one recorder to each person I wish to contact. I get much better results when I ask to speak with Cathy using my recorder with yellow tape on it. In my research, this is "Cathy's recorder." I recommend staying open in this arena, too.

- Hunches often guide me accurately. When I have the courage to *just do it*, whatever my gut is telling me; I often end up with beautiful results. When I force myself into situations because some "scientific" voice tells me I *should*, then I often get confusing results or nothing at all.

- Honoring my own experiences increases the openness in which inquiry can expand. When I can validate any experience, no matter how strange, I begin to "'see around corners" into realms which I could not have imagined had I remained closed to possibility. This requires that I not depend on anyone outside my experiment to validate me. When it comes from within, my work remains untouched by outside influences which may not know anything about it. At the same time, this practice allows me to honor the experiences of others, however strange those might seem. I've learned that "strangeness" just means that I've encountered something new; something which is perhaps worthy of investigation.

There are times when an inquiry from someone comes across as more a derogatory statement than a true question. Someone may ask me, for instance, "Don't you find it creepy to communicate with your deceased daughter?" Then I have no problem responding with another question, "What extreme measures would you take if it were possible for you to hear your child's voice again?" Although I seldom find it necessary to defend the choices I have made to use EVP and study its sometimes far-reaching possibilities, I have learned not to judge the limitations of those who ask such questions. I don't know what experiences have brought them to their inquiry, just as they likely do not know that *any* grieving mother might set out on *any* path that would allow her to speak with her child again.

I have to admit that sometimes I also wonder about what's going on with the person who has become so cynical as to want to discount what works for others. George Anderson has a whole chapter in *Walking in the Garden of Souls* about hope. He reminds us that loss of hope is "an unfortunate by-product" of losing someone we love to death. Then he reminds us that some will "... allow their hopelessness to become solid and immoveable, and it will become the labor of [others] to chip away at that stone until the light of hope can be seen through it."

Perhaps the cynics I encounter do face that horror of lost hope, face the long road of restoring it. The best I can do for them is to offer my story, along with one more quote from George Anderson: "Refusal to face the prospect of lost hope is a refusal to reconcile ourselves to the very circumstances we are sent here to experience and overcome." And I can also wish them hope.

Of course, if someone wishes to have a deeper or different understanding of *why* EVP works, or *how* it works, I invite that person to develop his or her own rigorous inquiry. For me, I have proof that EVP does work. And my research continues to develop understanding of the methods, circumstances and equipment which allow it to work best. That is my science. How will you construct yours?

Preparation for Making Contact

The group exercises which we use in our Recording Circle – Bridge to the Afterlife sessions, some of which have been covered in this book, will help you increase your chances for receiving EVP. When you record EVP, you are working within the spiritual realm. Like many talents or abilities, some people have more of a natural capacity to receive clear EVP than others. Consider all the psychics in the world. Though numerous, few have unique gifts. However, like every other skill or talent one might have, abilities can sharpen and increase with continued practice. This is especially true for being able to record EVP messages. By following certain procedures and exercises, you can increase your ability to connect with the spiritual world.

Many people think of using EVP for ghost investigations or just for fun, but my approach is restricted. I use it primarily for spiritual development purposes. I view this development in two separate parts. One must have both:

1. An interest in self-education for preparing us for our next phase of life;

2. Action stemming merely out of love and for unselfish reasons, from a desire to continue support for a loved one who is now in spirit.

Our Recording Circle – Bridge to the Afterlife group is unique because our mission does not include making contact just to the spiritual world in general, but reaching beyond the veil to a particular spirit of someone we love. Together with the aid of EVP, we work with both the physical and spiritual worlds to build a bridge to connect our world to the next.

For most of us, when we work with the spiritual world, we are opening ourselves up to an unknown reality. For this reason I consider it important to do a prayer of protection before recording. When you begin, you might visualize a bubble of white light, love and protection enveloping you.

To prepare yourself further, begin to think of yourself as consisting of three separate levels: body, mind and spirit. It is important to keep these three aspects in balance and attuned with each other. I find that by keeping these in sync, I feel able to raise my vibration rate to a higher level, making it easier to contact the spiritual world. I suggest that from now on, whenever you look at your physical form in a mirror, keep in mind these other two parts that make up your being, but which cannot be seen.

Following are more exercises which we use in our Recording Circle for alignment of the total being, taking each aspect of self in turn:

Body:

We often do a mild yoga stretching exercise: Stand with your legs approximately three feet apart, toes pointing forward, and arms at your sides. Relax your shoulders; keep your chin parallel to the floor. Your body weight should be evenly distributed between the toes and the heels, and from right to left. Straighten your legs and contract your thighs, keeping your knees unlocked and relaxed. Close your eyes while bringing your arms slowly up overhead and placing your palms flat together. Interlace your fingers while letting the index fingers point towards the ceiling. Inhale and stretch, imagining that you have an invisible string, attached to your index fingers and it is pulling you up toward the ceiling. Feel your vertebrae separate as the spine straightens. You may want to pretend that you are a puppet on a string while performing this exercise. Exhale slowly as your arms go downward, as if you are pushing the air down with them. Take a long and deep breath while visualizing a white, healing light flowing throughout your body. While inhaling, raise your arms upwards. Repeat this exercise three times.

Mind:

Mind-body activities are important and offer many tangible benefits, which in turn can heighten our level of inner awareness. The proper flow and balance of energy that you receive from proper breathing determines the state of our body-mind. It seems that a long time ago we forgot how to breathe. Too often, when we inhale, we only expand our lungs. Below is an exercise to refresh you in the proper method of breathing:

The three areas important to proper breathing includes the abdomen (or belly), the stomach, and the chest. In a standing position with your feet slightly apart, place one hand on your abdomen (below the navel), with the other hand on your stomach (above the navel). Inhale, allowing your abdomen to expand completely while keeping your stomach and chest at ease. Feel the breath move up and enter your stomach area as it expands upward from the filled abdomen. Now move your hand from your abdomen to your chest as the breath finally expands the chest fully. On the release, concentrate on doing just the opposite. Release breath from the chest first, then the stomach, then the abdomen. It is good to practice this exercise in front of a mirror until this type of breathing feels natural to you.

You can learn to lengthen and equalize your breaths by consciously letting the breaths become longer. Paying attention to your breathing can eliminate stress, helping to quiet the mind and bring about a deep state of relaxation. Repeat this exercise three times.

It is particularly important to remember proper breathing when we are going through stressful times in our life. I remember my priest saying this to us while we were awaiting Cathy's outcome at the hospital. He said, "Don't forget to breathe." Breathing is often the thing we forget to do adequately when we are under stress.

If you have ever been through natural childbirth, you were taught to use Lamaze breathing techniques. These exercises help to work you through your pain. By using our breath in much the same manner, we are able to work through the pain of any stressful situation. Negative emotions such as pain or stress can create mental blocks. I've learned from experience that they can limit my ability to contact the spiritual world. Breathing relaxes me to a point where contact becomes much more possible.

Spirit:
Meditation is just another tool to help you reach the level of consciousness that enables us to vibrate at a higher level. Meditation can also teach us how to manage stress and enhance one's overall physical and spiritual well-being. There are many kinds of meditation, so finding one which works best for you is a highly personal choice. I would suggest trying several different forms of meditations to see which one you prefer. There are books, video

and audiotapes, and all kinds of information on the Internet to educate you on the topic of meditation. You will find several very simple meditations in this book.

For the beginner, meditation with music and a visualization script might be the easiest form to follow. You can either sit in a comfortable chair or on the floor keeping your spine erect and body relaxed with your limbs uncrossed. If you choose to lie down, you may want support under your knees and head. Your body temperature may drop during meditation, so you may want to place a blanket around you. Before you begin your actual meditation, you might say your prayer of protection.

Choose music that you know will further relax you. I select something that reminds me of the person in spirit with whom I am trying to communicate. Play the music very softly, and visualize your loved one in your mind's eye or third eye, the point between the eyebrows. (I would suggest at this point you follow the meditation in the next section entitled "Contact through Self-Hypnosis.") You might want to start out with five minute meditations and work your way up to ten or fifteen minute meditations.

Now you are ready to record. When you turn on your recorder, you might want to say your name into it. Then ask a simple "yes" or "no" question that pertains to the spiritual world, addressing it to the person you love. Here's an example of how I might begin a recording with Cathy: "My name is Martha. I'm looking for my daughter who goes by the names of Cat, Cathy or Catherine." I then ask a question pertaining to her spiritual world such as, "Cat, do you have clouds in heaven?"

Now let the recorder run for five minutes. At the end of the interval, stop it and play back your recording. Listen to the recording at least twice before erasing it.

Always say a prayer for healing and thanksgiving when you finish your session. Good luck!

Contact through Self-Hypnosis

In our group, Recording Circle – Bridge to the Afterlife, we have found many procedures which work to help us attune ourselves to a greater possibility of communication with our loved ones. Following is a relaxation and visualization process that many of us use to build the bridge to our loved ones in their new existence. Some of us practice this ritual both upon waking in the morning and upon retiring at night. To further relax yourself at bedtime, try the exercise below between steps 3 and 4.

I suggest that you begin by using this entire process. Then perhaps experiment to see which parts or variations work best for you. Remember: Your imagination is the key to opening the door to the Other Side.

1. Play a song that reminds you of your loved one, perhaps a favorite. Place a picture of your loved one next to you.

2. Light a candle. Study the different colors of the flame.

3. Close your eyes and envision the flame in your mind's eye. (This is located in the center of your forehead, sometimes called the Third Eye.)

4. Focus on your breath. Breathe in the light of the candle. Breathe out and release any tensions or stress. Relax.

5. Notice that the light is now forming a beam, much like a laser light, flowing from your Third Eye.

6. Visualize the warmth of the glowing beam of light. Feel the light entering your body as you become lighter and lighter. Relax.

7. Notice that at the end of the beam you see the form of a person. As the person draws closer into the light, you can see it is your loved one. Feel your form rising, flowing toward your loved one and ending in an embrace.

8. Pay attention to every detail about your loved one. Study the face. Examine the clothing. Notice colors and fabrics.

9. Just be in this moment for a while, observing all details of the experience.

10. Focus on words forming in the beam of light from your Third Eye. What do you most want to know from your loved one? Now that the words are formed, send them in thought form to your loved one. You may want to express your love. Wait for a response.

11. Now ask your loved one whether he or she has a preference about how you communicate. If so, what is that preference? Wait for the answer.

12. Breathe in, breathe out. Relax. Enjoy this moment and feel the love that surrounds you both.

13. When you are ready, feel yourself embracing your loved ones again. Tell them you will be back soon.

At bedtime:
Do the first three steps above. Then make yourself comfortable lying down on your bed, and switch to this:

> From your mind's eye, notice that the light is moving toward your feet, forming a large ball of light just below the bottoms of your feet. You will feel the warmth of this light near your feet. **Inhale** a long, deep breath. Now visualize the light entering your feet. Notice that your feet begin to truly relax as the light flows into them. Now **exhale**, and as you do, feel your feet sink into the bed. **Inhale** and visualize the warm, white light flowing slowly up your legs and into your knees. **Exhale** and release any stress or discomfort in the lower part of your legs. **Inhale** and visualize this warm light flowing slowly through your thighs and into your hips. **Exhale** and release any stress still remaining in your legs. **Inhale** slowly and deeply, and then **exhale** slowly. Ask these lighted areas to relax completely. Notice that your entire body is sinking deeper and deeper into your bed, and that a smile is slowly spreading itself across your face. You can feel this smile all over.
>
> **Inhale** again, seeing the light flowing further upward, through your abdomen, filling your internal organs with this warm and healing light. You're breathing the light into your intestines, your liver and kidneys, your bladder, your stomach, your lungs, your lymphatic and endocrine systems. You can feel the nurturing

light surrounding and penetrating your heart. **Exhale** deeply and fully release any stress, any uncomfortable thoughts, emotions or fears. Notice that you are feeling completely relaxed, beginning to feel a slight floating sensation.

Inhale deeply as you visualize the light flowing into your arms and down to your fingertips. **Exhale** slowly as all the lighted areas of your body sink deeper and deeper. Feel the light extending its healing energy throughout your body.

Inhale again and notice the light extending through your neck and into your head, your eyes, nose, mouth and tongue. Feel it in your ears, flowing through your brain. **Exhale** and release all your fears and worries. Feel yourself sinking deeper and deeper as you find yourself completely relaxed from head to toe.

Now begin again with Step 4 above and continue through the end of the exercise. It is important to continue to focus on your breath, which will keep you relaxed but away from the brink of sleepiness.

Journaling Dreams

I have found a dream journal to be another important building block on that bridge to the spiritual world. You can purchase an inexpensive notebook or a more elaborate journal especially for dreams. Either will serve the purpose. Keep either this journal or a recorder next to your bed.

Before you fall to sleep, repeat to yourself, "I will remember any important dreams." Perhaps you want to close your eyes and visualize a blackboard. See yourself writing on the blackboard, "I will remember my dreams." Do this three times. Notice that the letters on this blackboard seem to glow, like they're fluorescent. See your loved one standing beside the blackboard, smiling and saying to you, "I will help you to remember your dreams."

When you awaken from a dream in the night, it is important to get at least the framework of the dream recorded. If you're using a journal, you may jot down a few words to help you remember the entire dream later. If using a recorder, you can say the few key words into it. Notice things, such as who was there, what was happening and distinct or unusual features.

Of course, if you share your sleeping space with another, you may have to leave your bed to complete either of these tasks. The key here is to disrupt your sleep as little as possible, but to still have the key aspects of the dream available in the morning.

If I fail to do this note-taking task, I usually have great difficulty writing the entire dream when I awaken. Most of my spiritual dreams seem to occur before 3:00 A.M., and if I awaken to write the entire dream, then my husband Don and my cat Sarah Jane don't really appreciate the disruption if I write in my journal or talk into a recorder for an extended period of time. And I'm fully awakened if I've taken time to record it all.

When I awaken in the morning, my first or second task is to write down in detail any dreams which occurred before waking. Then I sit with my journal or recorder and review the notes which came during the night. This usually takes me right back to the dream, where I'm experiencing it fully once again. As with any dreams which occurred later in the night, I now record the early dreams in full detail, noticing colors, textures, activities, what was said, who was there, etc. I've heard someone describe this as "catching the tail of the dream before it submerges back into the ocean." By preserving the "tail" briefly during the night, I can usually pull the entire whale back from the depths and examine it in detail. I hope this works as effectively for you!

Beginning to Record EVP

Although my recording of Cathy's voice began inadvertently through my computer, I have certainly learned a great deal about equipment, software and methods which enhance the process. I want to share with you the document which AA-EVP publishes about how to record EVP, with my comments added. Before I start with the "head stuff," I'll share the prayer that we use to connect our hearts to the process. We join in saying this as we begin each group recording session every:

Invocation

May Beings of Light enfold me.
May Beings of Light uphold me.
May Beings of Light sustain me.
May Beings of Light encircle me.
May Beings of Light protect me.
May I forever abide in the ever-expanding and overwhelming
   brilliance of Love and Truth.
                    Amen.

Although we always ask for light to surround us in this process, I want to state that it is more for focus than for "safety." My experience has borne out what many others have realized: There is truly only goodness on the Other Side. The "darkness" that we perceive is actually trapped here with us, within us, in the human reality.

Again, George Anderson provides considerable insight into this. His book *Walking in the Garden of Souls* has an entire chapter on it, entitled "See—No Evil." He reminds us of the very human propensity to imagine that evil is outside us. (The well-known theologian Karen Armstrong also wrote about this in her book, *The Origin of Satan*.) Anderson says that a dark, supernatural force is "so easy to be blamed when we don't want to face our own failings on earth."

George further reminds us that it's truly sad when humans believe, and our media too often portray, a so-called evil force with more power than God. "There are no demons," he says, "only manifestations of our own fear of the evil that exists here on earth." So we invoke the light when we do EVP to keep us from our very own fears.

Now, here's some instruction to help you record your own EVP:

Recording Entity Voices

EVP is the appearance of intelligible voices on recording media that have no physical explanation. They are thought to originate from deceased people, which is the primary reason that people first began to experiment. Others study EVP to better understand how and why it works, and to improve experiment techniques. Recording devices need not be expensive. As in any field of interest, some people are better at it than others. With patience, perseverance and good listening techniques, anyone should be able to record and hear EVP messages.

While conventional EVP wisdom says that no one is likely to record a message on the first try, I've had guests in my home succeed on their first attempt. I've learned that no hard-and-fast rules apply, and that persistence is usually necessary.

Voice Characteristics

Recorded voices may be very quiet and are often difficult to hear and understand at first. Most EVP experimenters say that they have developed "an ear" for this by learning to distinguish voices from background noise. Once this is learned, voices can often be recognized as male or female, young or old. Messages usually last two seconds or less, and are most often two to four words. The words may be spoken very quickly, and there is often a distinctive cadence to EVP voices.

Basic Equipment Needs

Recorders:
EVP has been recorded on all types of equipment. If you're tape recording, it's best to use a cassette tape deck with mechanical controls which allow easy, repeated review of the voices. Be sure the recorder has a counter. People report success when recording EVP with such devices as digital note takers, telephone answering machines and computers with Windows Media Player or similar software.

Microphones:
The built-in microphone on a portable tape recorder tends to cause very noisy tapes, so we've found it best to use an external microphone. We suggest that you use this to record both questions you are asking

and any EVP responses you might get. This helps recorded messages to have more meaning and seem less random.

Headphones:
Since EVP voices are frequently not loud, many voices may be missed unless headphones are used. The earmuff-type, which completely covers the ears, is best.

Tape:
Any low-noise, high sensitivity tape may be used. A tape no longer than sixty minutes (thirty minutes on each side) is recommended.

Speaker(s):
Separate speakers are not necessary, but they are good to have, especially if you wish to play your recordings back to a group of people.

I like to connect my recorder to two small speakers (which do not have to be expensive). While in my bathroom putting on my make-up in the mornings, I keep a small paper pad handy with a pen and list the recorder I am using, the folder number, and the minutes and seconds. For a tape recorder you would list the number registered on the recorder's counter and what you heard. By doing this you can save yourself time, and trouble, without getting "burned out" from the process of downloading recordings into the computer. You can use your little speakers anywhere, in the kitchen, your office or workshop.

General Recording Procedure

Scheduling:
Always tape when your energy level is highest! Entities will speak on tape at any time of day or night. In the beginning, however, it is advisable to record at a regular time and place. By doing this, entities will learn when and where they can count on your availability. Once this connection is established, you become more able to collect EVP any time, anywhere. It's okay to provide background sounds, but it's important that you be aware of these when listening back to your recordings so that you will recognize which sounds are natural and which are EVP. Keep your recordings short. You will want to listen to each part of the recording very carefully, and this takes time.

Background Sound Source:

We have found that entities use sounds in the environment to help form EVP messages. Most recording situations have some background sounds, but you may wish to add sound to your recording environment. A fan, a radio or running water will work. Some people use foreign language radio or audio tapes. The entity will sometimes re-modulate your voice or other sounds in the environment. Please note that some people believe that background sound is not necessary. This is a point of frequent discussion, so find what's best for you.

Recording:

Vocalize your comments during an EVP session. Many experimenters begin with a short prayer and an invitation to friends on the Other Side to participate in the experiment. It can be helpful to begin the experiment by speaking your name and the date. We've found that entities will often come through as soon as the recorder is turned on. These beginning messages are often the loudest, so it's a good idea to turn on the recorder and wait a few seconds before announcing yourself, then ask questions. Remember to record your questions, then wait awhile before asking more, giving the entities time to respond.

Some experimenters make an appointment with the intended entity the day before during prayer or meditation. Some also provide feedback before the session so that the entities will know how the last experiment went. Although our members try all kinds of methods, devices, and energy sources, it is not necessary to record in the dark, nor with any specific accoutrements. *I've always loved the energy of crystals, so I use those for my recording, along with items I've described elsewhere. You might want to try putting written questions in the EVP experiment area the day before. We are told the entities will read these and may respond accordingly.*

Playback:

The paranormal voice is not heard until playback. Experimenters report that the voices tend to become stronger and clearer as they gain in experience. At first, the voices may sound like mere whispers. Voices may not be captured in every session. Hearing the voices is a learned ability, so be persistent. The entities seem to learn through practice, too, coming through more frequently and loudly over time.

Voice Classifications:
Class A voice recordings are those that can be heard and understood by most people. Class B voices can be heard over a speaker, but not everyone will agree as to what is said. Class C voices can only be heard with headphones and may be hard to understand. Class B or C voice recordings may have only one or two clearly discernible words. Loudness does not constitute a Class A recording.

Keeping a Log:
Maintaining a record of your recording results can be very helpful. Include the date, time, place on the counter or folder where the message is stored, a notation of the message itself and the question asked.

Weather:
Experimenters report that they feel weather may affect recording results. Our website, www.aaevp.com has geomagnetic and solar reports, along with a link for moon phase information. You may want to include this information in your log to begin to notice whether this plays a part in your recording success.

EVP on the Reverse Side of Audio Tape

EVP experimenters have discovered voices on the reverse direction of the sound track. After you have reviewed your tape for voices in the usual way, you can listen to it again while playing it backwards. Your voice will be heard in reverse, and EVP voices may be heard as if they are being played forward. This is easiest with sound editing software for your computer. We like Adobe Audition program for this, available at www.adobe.com/products/audition/main.html. [This program was known as "Cool Edit" before Adobe purchased the software. Audacity is a free audio program at http://audacity.sourceforge.net/.]

Reverse-play cassette decks are also available. Alternatively, it is possible to "break" an auto-reversing tape player so that, when it reverses the tape to play Side B, it plays Side A backwards.

It is very important to remember that your voice heard in reverse is not an EVP. When some words are heard in reverse they naturally form other words. You may listen to your own voice in reverse and find it to be making some kind of statement that is different from your forward voice. This phenomenon is called Reverse Speech and is not EVP and should not be confused with EVP.

Computer Recording

You can substitute a computer for the audio recorder if you wish. Your computer will need to have an audio input jack, speaker and head-phone jacks, and a sound player software of some form. More recent Windows versions come with a sound recorder application that will work. A sound editor program is most popular for this option because it allows for easy analysis of the sound track.

It is possible to record directly with your computer, using the sound editor as a recorder, or to record with a tape or digital recorder, then play it back and edit it on your computer. This requires a microphone which is connected to your computer.

In addition, you can download a free software program called EVPMaker from www.stefanbion.de/evpmaker/. This was developed by Stefan Bion of the German VTF (Vereins Fur Tonbandstimmenfor-schung), an organization like ours in Europe. This program is different from a sound editor. It uses random controlled phoneme synthesized from "raw" sound tracks to conduct a form of EVP experiment on the computer. The phonemes, which are really just bits of sound, are reas-sembled into a new sound track based on a random number process. That random process thought to be where the EVP is caused.

The AA-EVP web site includes a caution concerning EVPMaker. First, it is important to use a very short sample rate because the default sample rate may leave enough of the raw sound track intact to produce normal words. Second, the experimenter should be aware that other experimenters have reported an extraordinarily high percentage of messages that are negative in content. Thus, it is recommended that a person who is new to EVP begin first with an audio recorder, and learn more about what EVP is and is not before trying EVPMaker.

Questions?

These instructions include the most common techniques for recording EVP. They will help anyone get started. We have found that EVP may occur with any technology that will record voice. With this in mind, it should be clear that there are no hard-and-fast rules in EVP. Should you need help, please contact Tom and Lisa Butler, AA-EVP Direc-tors, at their website: www.aaevp.com. Membership information is available there also.

Too Where You Are

Cathy, age seven

I cannot watch Josh Groban sing. I experience too much cognitive dissonance because a kid that young cannot possibly sing like he does. Yet I do love to listen to him, often in my car. Today I'm listening to a song that my secret pal from church sent to me after Cathy's death, one which still brings tears to my eyes:

> "Who can say for certain
> Maybe you're still here
> I feel you all around me
> Your memory's so clear
> Deep in the stillness
> I can hear you speak"

I think about the magnificent truth of these words. The discovery of EVP has indeed created and maintained an opportunity for me to feel her around me, to hear Cathy speak, often and clearly. And it is indeed the deep stillness that sends to me her voice much as it was when she was alive.

My hands grip the wheel a little tighter, and when I notice my fingers beginning to hurt, I chuckle to myself. I've been looking at the clouds again, those high, fluffy ones. They always seem to pull at me, and there's part of me that wants to float right up there and join Cathy. So I guess my hands are working hard to keep me here. Josh's voice soars,

> "Fly me up to where you are
> Beyond the distant star
> I wish upon tonight
> To see you smile
> If only for awhile
> To know you're there
> A breath a way's not far too where you are."

I feel a smile spreading through me. What a rare and beautiful comfort it has been to know that my Cat is alright and in a beautiful place. In dreams that I have had, that Rachel and others have had, we have indeed been flown to where Cathy is now. I wipe my eyes and smile, grateful for the experiences I have had, thankful to know that it is truly "not far too where you are."

We Figured it Out

Cathy in 2000. Her first car.

Genuinely concerned people have asked me to contact a mother who has just recently lost a child. They hope our story of the "Big Circle" will ease her pain. However, I feel this is not the appropriate time. We all have to go through the different stages of the grieving process that this sort of tragedy throws us into. The person must first be in a mental state to accept EVP as a means of continuing communications with the child. These communications are not the same as when they were in the physical and sometimes can be very frustrating. Although EVP is not a replacement for what we had in the physical, there are few other alternatives or options available to us for continuing after-death communications. EVP is better than no communication at all from your loved one in spirit. Hearing that familiar voice (even if only a word or two) is better then facing the reality of knowing that you will never again hear that precious voice while in the physical.

I do not understand the reason so many people prefer to remain in the "Dark Ages" when it comes to EVP. My sister Ginny's theory is for some people if they can't see it, taste it, feel it, or buy it, (or …get it off eBay!) then it does not exist.

If you have lost children, remember Cathy's words during the reading with George Anderson. He began, "Your daughter is telling you and the other parents in the room, 'I know that you feel now that you are carrying a heavy cross; but I want you to know right now that you will find resolve.'"

Perhaps the phenomena taking place with our "Big Circle" is the "*resolve*" to which Cathy was referring during this reading.

I looked up the word, "*resolve*," in the dictionary to see if I could figure out how this word relates to our story. Indeed, I discovered these definitions:

1. **To change or convert:** Will our group change how people relate to the death experience and after-death communication?
2. **To find solution:** Will we find a solution or a more in-depth understanding of the wrenching question, "Why me"?
3. **To bring to a successful conclusion:** Will we be able to release ourselves from the unnecessary feeling of guilt, allowing us to better comprehend the bigger picture from this experience?
4. **To cause reduction (have an inflammation, for example) or to render parts visible and distinct; to melt or dissolve:** Can we help aid in the reduction of pain from grief by sharing our after-death communications with others who have experienced a loss?

Clearly, the word, "resolve," is loaded with meaningfulness, and Cathy understood its relevance.

As Braden (Vicki Talbott's son) once told his mother through mediums, and Cathy told me in a dream for Karen Mossey from her son, Rob, *"You'll figure it out."*

After completing this last page of the book, I envisioned a white light of love and protection surrounding me. Turning on my recorder, I posed this question: "Cathy, how do you and The Big Circle feel about the book?" Playing back the recording, I could hear Cathy's voice saying, *"Thank you, Mom,"* and a male voice followed her voice with a clear *"thank you."*

AA-EVP Membership Form

Membership in the Association is open to anyone 18 and older. Annual dues are:

0 Member $30   All services for one year
0 * International Member not using Email $38   All services for one year
0 Sustaining member $100 Member + name listed in
                                        NewsJournal

* International member **not receiving NewsJournal via email as a PDF file.**

All dues must be in US Denomination. Please make checks payable to AA-EVP.

Mail check and form to: AA-EVP, PO Box 13111, Reno, NV 89514

Name_____

Email Address (Optional)_____

Address_____

City/State/Zip code_____ Country_____

Do you wish to be on the Cross-country list?_____

Do you wish to include your physical address?_____

Do you wish to include your email address?_____

Do you wish to receive the NewsJournal via email _____
or, via the Postal Service?_____

On the Other Side, tell us a little about yourself, and if you record and what techniques you like to use.

Member Profile (Please check what best describes your interest in EVP)
[ ] I record on a regular basis.
[ ] I plan to begin recording.
[ ] I have a scientific background and am interested in working in R&D for EVP.
[ ] None of the above. I have an interest in EVP and its evidence for survival.

I understand that the cross-country list should not be used for commercial purposes or the furtherance of personal causes. By indicating that I want to share my name and address with others through the cross-country list, I realize this is a private list and I agree that other names on the list will not be given to anyone who is not on the list. I also understand that my name will be removed from the list and my membership in AA-EVP will be terminated if I violate this agreement.

Signed _____Date_____

You can now submit a membership form online at aaevp.com. You can also submit your membership dues online via PayPal. You will be guided to do so after filling out the online membership form. The AA-EVP is a 501 (c)(3) organization. Funds in excess of dues are tax deductible in the USA.

There is No Death and There are No Dead

By
Tom and Lisa Butler
Directors of the AA-EVP

$18.00 when printed in the USA

Number of copies: _____ X $18.00

Subtotal: _____

Nevada State Sales Tax: _____ (Nevada Residence only)

Shipping and Handling: _____

Total Enclosed: _____ **Please make check to: AA-EVP**

Shipping and Handling Charges

	Media Mail	First Class	International
First book:	$4.00	$6.00	$10.00
Each additional:	$1.00	$2.00	$10.00

Please attach a list with instructions if you would like signed copies of this book.

Mail book(s) to: Name: _____

Street address: _____

City, State, Zip: _____

Telephone Number (Optional): _____

Email Address (Optional): _____

Contact aaevpsupport@aol.com if you have questions.

Send order to AA-EVP, PO Box 13111, Reno, NV 89507 or go to
http://book.aaevp.com and order using PayPal.

For copies of *I'm Still Here*

Price: $17.95 each when printed in the USA *

Number of copies: _____ X $17.95

Subtotal: _____

Georgia State Sales Tax: _____ (Georgia Residence only)

Shipping and Handling: _____

Total Enclosed: _____
Please make check to: Martha Copeland

Shipping and Handling Charges

	Media Mail	First Class	International
First book:	$4.00	$6.00	$10.00
Each additional:	$1.00	$2.00	$10.00

Please attach a list with instructions if you would like signed copies of this book.

Mail book(s) to: Name: _____

Street address: _____

City, State, Zip: _____

Telephone Number (Optional): _____

Email Address (Optional): _____

Contact catsstillhere@yahoo.com if you have questions.

Send order to A Martha Copeland
#191
6555 Sugarloaf Parkway, Suite 307
Duluth, GA 30097

More information about this book is available at:
www.evpcommunications.com

* Please note that price is subject to change

Printed in the United States
40113LVS00006B/334